MW00532451

THE SHIP THAT ROCKED THE WORLD

Also by Tom Lodge
Beyond the Great Slave Lake
Success Without Goals
Circles, Tom Lodge becoming Umi

As Umi
Footprints in the Snow
The River and the Raven
Enlightenment Guaranteed
God is a Dancer
The Diamond Sutra with Umi

THE SHIP THAT ROCKED THE WORLD

**How Radio Caroline Defied the Establishment,
Launched the British Invasion and
Made the Planet Safe for Rock and Roll**

TOM LODGE

WITH A FOREWORD BY
STEVEN VAN ZANDT

Bartleby Press
Washington • Baltimore

Copyright © 2010 by Tom Lodge
All rights reserved. No part of this book may be used or
reproduced in any form whatsoever without written permission,
except in the case of brief quotations embodied in critical
reviews and articles.

Printed in the United States of America

Published and distributed by:

Bartleby Press

8600 Foundry Street
Mill Box 2043
Savage, Maryland 20763
800-953-9929
www.BartlebythePublisher.com

Library of Congress Cataloging-in-Publication Data

Lodge, Tom, 1936-
 The ship that rocked the world : how Radio Caroline defied
the establishment, launched the British invasion and made the
planet safe for rock and roll / Tom Lodge.
    p. cm.
 ISBN 978-0-910155-82-3 (hardcover)
 1. Radio Caroline. 2. Pirate radio broadcasting--Great Britain--
History. 3. Popular music radio stations--Great Britain--History.
4. Umi, 1936- I. Title.
 HE8697.65.G7L63 2010
 384.540941--dc22
                                    2009049431

In memory of my friend,
Christopher C. Peterson
1954-2009

Contents

Foreword

This is an adventure story, so let's get that straight right up front.

Ronan O'Rahilly and his gang of rogues, renegades and roustabouts had little intention of making history and every intention of making trouble. Of course, what they pulled off ended up doing both. And along the way incurring the class-conscious, self righteous and occasionally dangerously irrational wrath of Her Majesty's Government, which considered everything from illegally sinking the ship (it actually had a plan), to assassination (which, incredibly, it almost did).

And for what high crimes against the Empire was all this wrath in defense of, you ask?

Nuclear threat?

Economic subversion?

Spreading the Plague perhaps?

No, sorry. On Radio Caroline, they performed the singularly treasonous act of playing rock and roll records to an audience that couldn't hear them anywhere else.

So in other words, the British government's response was only a bit more extreme than most of our parents!

We were lucky in America. We had great radio from the mid-fifties on.

Our horrified, unsuspecting, long-suffering hard-working mothers and fathers witnessed the birth of a new species—the Teenager— who came in such numbers that they couldn't be exterminated and quickly took over.

And they brought their own soundtrack with them.

By the way, destiny would play a role in the flourishing of that soundtrack in two big ways.

When William Paley and CBS introduced the 33 1/3 RPM 12 inch Long Player (LP) in 1948, whose more durable Vinylite plastic would ultimately replace the 78-RPM's very breakable shellac, his chief rival General David Sarnoff at RCA had to invent something to compete. It would be the 45RPM 7 inch single (6 7/8 actually) introduced in 1949.

This would coincide with a musician's strike (they assumed records would put them out of business!) which forced record companies to produce more children's records and—here's the thing—tiny portable phonograph machines to go with them. Thusly enabling kids, soon to be teenagers, the ability to play the records they wanted, when they wanted, in the privacy of their own rooms, as opposed to the colossal console in the middle of the living room which was closely policed by one's parents.

This teenage technology came along just in time because their sound track turned out to be an unholy combination of Hillbilly trash, Blues shouters, and Gospel fugitives that some lunatic DJ named Alan Freed was calling Rock and Roll ("wasn't that what black people called sex?!"). Surely this would never have survived (or even seen the light of day) in adultsville.

And then, as if by Satanic wizardry—and maybe the reference to the Plague was accurate after all—it hit the Mother Country like a wayward tsunami.

And boy were they ready for it.

It was a country bursting at the seams with frustrated teenagers waiting for a post-World War, black and white life to explode into wide-screen Technicolor. Loudly.

And just in case you think frustrated is too strong a word, keep in mind it was those conservative, well-behaved English teenagers that, upon witnessing Bill Haley and the Comets "Rock Around The Clock" as it opened the classic film *Blackboard Jungle*, literally ripped the seats out of the theater. They did so for one simple reason. No one had ever heard rock and roll at the proper volume before—you know—loud. And out of those gigantic speakers spilled liberation.

Freedom baby!

That's what this music was all about. And the explosion of liberation came from the unlikely barrels of the cannons aboard Radio Caroline's Danish passenger ferry, the MV *Fredericia*, anchored three and a half miles out to sea in International waters. It broadcast the British Invasion back to Britain and gave it the strength it would need to cross the ocean.

Every ocean.

And without them...well, unless "How Much Is That Doggie In The Window" turns you on, you don't even want to think about it.

So settle back me hearties and let old Tom Lodge spin you a tale about a band of pirates that never made it to the Caribbean, but against all odds made it to New Jersey.

And accidentally saved my life.

— Steven Van Zandt

Acknowledgments

R ight at the start, I wish to thank Jonathan Myer for first printing my personal Radio Caroline photographs on his web page, *www.offshoreradio.co.uk*. It was because of his encouragement that I began to write this book. He provided even more inspiration by adding some of my personal experiences on Radio Caroline North and South to his web pages.

Peter Moore's strong, continuous support of Radio Caroline has kept the dream going, even to this present day. It was Peter who invited me to deejay once again, back in the 1990s, on a few of their one-month broadcasts..

Thank you, Tom Maguire, for finding typos hidden inside the pages.

I also want to give a big thank you to Christopher C.

Peterson, a close friend who has been very involved in the unfolding of this important story.

I am grateful to my publisher, Jeremy Kay and his editor Lateef Padgett. Both have inspired me to delve deep into my memories and bring out aspects of this adventure that were personal and special.

Thank you to David Kindred, *www.kindred-spirit.co.uk*, for some of the photographs used in this book.

The photo on page 87 of the five deejays on Caroline South was originally from Essex County Newspapers and reprinted in *Offshore Radio* published by Iceni Enterprises.

And now a big Thank You to the Stillpoint Zen Community, where I am now living. Thanks for the support, the Sangha, *www.umiji.org*.

Prologue

The music and the fans' support made us blind to the forces that were collecting to wipe us off the map. The Royal Navy's appearance and the continual anti-Caroline TV reports from the British government were just part of the excitement. We were having fun and were willing to play the game to the end. It wasn't until a few years ago, long after my microphone fell silent, that I learned how near we had come to a violent end. I was visiting my friend Gary Hall in Vancouver, British Columbia.

He took me downtown to a large, nondescript building. We went upstairs and through some dark corridors into a plain-looking office. Sitting at a desk was a middle-aged, stocky man with thick lens glasses. "This is Colin Hall," said Gary. We shook hands.

"Gary says that you were on Radio Caroline," said Colin.

"Yes, I was," I replied. "It was some adventure."

"What year was that?" Colin asked.

"1964 to 1967. It was the initial stage, when rock and roll was an enigma to Britain."

"Yes, I know," Colin replied. "I nearly blew you guys out of the water."

"What?"

Gary spoke up. "Colin was with MI5, you know, the English version of the CIA."

"MI5? No way! Where were you stationed at the time?" I asked.

"Southern Ireland."

"Where in Southern Ireland?"

"I can't tell you that."

"When was that?"

"About October 1966."

"Yes, I was onboard then. What happened?"

Colin got up from the desk and walked away. It seemed as if he were avoiding me. I really wanted to hear this story, but was worried he would clam up. I stayed quiet, but followed him attentively.

Without looking at me he said, "I got a phone call from Brigadier General George Dixon. Just out of the blue." He paused and looked at me. I could see his eyes sitting behind his thick lenses. "The general came right to the point. 'Colin,' he said. 'I have an assignment for you.'"

He paused for a moment. "The general was from the old school, he had been to some posh English boarding school and he had that accent."

Colin put on the upper class English accent, "'You know

that ship off the coast that is broadcasting this rock and roll noise? Well, I want you to take a helicopter and some of the SAS boys and raid them. Stop them from broadcasting. Get the crystal out of their transmitter and whatever else it takes to get that nuisance silenced. We have instructions from high-up that this has to stop. Okay, old boy?'"

I listened intently to Colin's tale. It was quite amazing. The SAS is the Special Air Service, a secret British attack unit, a military SWAT team.

"At first I was taken aback," Colin continued, "but I composed myself and explained the situation to the general."

"'You see, sir, all of the SAS boys are between eighteen and twenty-two. They are ardent fans of Radio Caroline. I could not ask them to do that. Radio Caroline has been on-the-air long enough now that it's loved by so many people. The boys couldn't do that. I'm sorry, sir. It just wouldn't work. It's an impossible job.'"

Colin stopped and looked directly at me, "I was expecting the full broadside. After all, he was a tough, old general. But to my surprise, he wasn't upset."

"'Damn it, old boy!' he said. 'But yes, I think I see your point. I believe you are right. Thank you, Colin. Bye.'"

Colin smiled. "That was it. We left you alone."

I was stunned. I finally spoke, "I'm grateful that you did. Thanks."

Since then I have often wondered how many more near misses we may have had. I guess life is just a series of near misses, otherwise I wouldn't be telling you this story now.

CHAPTER 1

My New Home on the Horizon

I t was time for a pint on this damp, dull London day. Of course, in March 1964, the rest of England was also damp and dull. It was a society filled with stiff and snobby adults who spurned rock and roll, a society where short hair was mandatory. The class structure of a thousand years was ingrained and prevented the young people of the working class from moving out of their social prisons; it also kept the youth of the upper class from letting loose and having fun. Another barrier was the regulatory system that only permitted the government-owned BBC radio to broadcast in England. Working together, these forces were strangling a nation of fifty million people. Back then, there was definitely no Carnaby Street.

I dropped into a pub on the King's Road. As I entered, I squinted in its low lights and smoke-filled air. It was decorated with dark paneling and swirling engraved glass, the familiar and stiff Victorian style that was the standard of the time. The radio behind the bar played some BBC Light Programme music, the sound of which made me shudder. It was "What Did Delaware" by Perry Como. I took off my wet coat and walked up to the bartender wiping down the bar.

"That's pretty awful music."

"So?" said the bartender. "That's the best we got."

A young fella sitting at the bar next to me piped up with an Irish accent, "Don't you be worrying, we'll soon be putting out the finest rock and roll and you can say 'goodbye' to that stuff."

"How's that?" I asked.

"We got a ship off the coast and in a few days we'll be on-the-air."

"Yeah?" I said. "That's great! Do you need any more deejays?"

"You're in radio?"

"I freelance for the CBC. But I'd rather be a deejay, playing rock and roll music."

"Well, that's real good, when can you start?"

"Whenever you want," I said extending my hand for him to shake. "The name's Tom Lodge."

"Good. I'm Ronan O'Rahilly," he said, taking my hand in a firm grip.

That was how I moved from the Canadian Broadcasting Corporation to Radio Caroline. At the time, I was living in Ealing, London with my wife Jeanine and my three boys, Tommy, Brodie and Lionel. They were ages four, three and one. Since my income from the CBC was not enough to cover our expenses, I also washed dishes at Earl's Court Exhibition Center. For a few extra peanuts, I did a stint of singing on BBC TV. After four years in England, I missed the free-flowing music that I heard in Canada. But now I had this opportunity.

Before moving to England I lived in Canada's Northwest Territories, first in Hay River and then in Yellowknife. In Hay River I ran a fishing business on the southern shore of Great Slave Lake. This business involved cutting holes through the ice and catching fish with nets at temperatures reaching sixty degrees below zero.

One day when I was eighteen, the ice broke apart, sending me, my companion and our three sled dogs drifting across one hundred miles of open water. My companion died, but some native trappers rescued me.

About three years later I returned to Hay River with my partner, Joe Boschman. At this time, Northern Canada was still in its Wild West phase. In that spirit, one night Joe took off with all of our fishing equipment and left me broke and stranded. After I recovered from the shock, my wife Jeannine and I struggled our way further north to the gold mine town of Yellowknife where I got a job in a mine.

After a year at the gold mine, I met some CBC government officials who were going to open a new CBC radio station in Yellowknife.

"Hey," I said. "Give me a job!"

I would do anything to get me away from the gold mine. Much to my surprise, I was hired, and after a month was doing the morning show. I had no experience behind the microphone. But I had been an avid listener to those great American deejays of the 1950s. They were my mentors. So there I was, each morning playing rock and roll. I was in my element.

Soon I began yearning for a bigger world than Yellow-knife and put in a request to the CBC head office to be a foreign correspondent in London, England. After a few weeks the news came; I was assigned to two of the CBC's news programs, *Assignment* and *Project*.

As fast as we could organize ourselves, we boarded a ship for England. Once we arrived in London, I went story-chasing for the CBC. With a tape recorder and microphone in hand, with youthful enthusiasm and boundless energy, I interviewed the likes of Sean Connery and Lord Bertram Russell. I interviewed Connery when he was filming *The Frightened City*, in his pre-James Bond days. I found Lord Bertram Russell, philosopher and mathematician, sitting on the sidewalk outside of the British Defense building in London, protesting the atomic bomb. I was creating a collection of great stories for the CBC. To support this work, I made my home into a small recording studio.

But until that day, when I walked into that pub on the Kings Road, I had absolutely no idea how moving to England would really change my life. I had already crossed the Atlantic eight times on ocean liners, then the cheapest way to travel, and I loved the ocean. And now I had a chance to indulge in two of my greatest passions, being on the radio and being on the ocean. What an amazing gift.

"Yes!" I shouted as I rode home on the London Underground. I ran into our house and grabbed Jeanine and hugged her. I told her the news. She was happy to hear about this unexpected opportunity that had dropped from the sky, and so that evening we all celebrated with a bottle of wine for Jeanine and me, and jelly and ice cream for the boys. After our meal, I romped on the floor with my sons, rolling over and over, wrestling and throwing them in the air. It felt so good to have Jeanine totally in agreement with my going out onto the ship. I have often thought since what a perfect friend and lover Jeanine was. She supported my adventure fully, even though she knew I would be away for weeks at a time.

I traveled by train from London to the port of Felixstowe, Suffolk, where Radio Caroline was anchored three and a half miles off the coast. At that time, any sea beyond three miles from the coast was considered international waters and a safe place from the laws of England. There was a small fishing boat waiting for me when I reached the dock. The skipper, with a strong Suffolk accent, welcomed me aboard. With the drone of the engine and the splashing of the waves against the bow, we headed out to the ship.

There was the ship, my future home on the horizon, a ship with a mast that looked far too big. Yet she sat queen-like, steady in the water. As our small boat bounced closer to her, I could hear the rumble of engines. Once alongside, our small boat rode up and down with the waves while the ship rested steadily, solid and secure. A new adventure was beginning.

As we jiggled and rocked with the waves, I waited for the right moment to jump aboard. I was greeted by deejay

Simon Dee, a tall, sandy-haired and serious-looking man. He took me for a tour of the ship. But in that first moment, as my feet hit the steel deck with a ring, the smell of the ship, the smell of new paint, diesel oil and salt flooded through me. I was immersed with memories of other ships—memories of the ship I rode when I was four, fleeing Hitler's armies; then the ship I rode when I was eighteen, immigrating to Canada to be a cowboy; and finally at twenty, the ship I sailed on from New York to win back Jeanine, the girl of my dreams.

Embedded in these memories was also the sour odor of other people's vomit. But this was the ocean. This was freedom. This was where there was no end to the water. This was where the horizon melted into the sky and the air tinged my lungs. This was the release from all of society's confinements.

MV *Caroline* with the tender, *Essex Girl*

Radio Caroline broadcast from the ship MV *Fredericia*, a Danish passenger ferry that Ronan had bought and rigged up as a radio station in the Irish port of Greenore. She was an elegant lady with a large galley where we ate, sorted new record releases, played cards and swapped the latest gossip.

The Wijsmuller Company, a Dutch shipping company, was employed by Ronan to run the ship. They supplied a captain, a chief engineer, a cook and a crew of three sailors. Their main function was to keep us anchored and safe, to keep the electrical generator running, make our meals, keep the ship clean and to continually paint the ship. The salt of the ocean is corrosive to the hull and other metal parts; as such, the ship needed constant care.

On our side, we had on staff a broadcast engineer. The broadcast engineer was responsible for taking care of the studio equipment, the transmitter and the link to the mast. But most important to my mind was the deejays; we were a group of young, enthusiastic adventurers who were hungry for music. We took care of the record library, with its floor to ceiling shelves of vinyl LPs and 45s, and the studio setup, with its records and posters. We also made sure that every moment was fun.

There were two distinct cultures sequestered and confined to the limited spaces of this ship. There were the Dutch-speaking, methodical, down-to-earth, efficient sailors and the English-speaking, pie-in-the-sky, excited and enthusiastic deejays. Sometimes we complemented each other and sometimes we clashed. The law of the sea is that the captain is king. But this was different. We were not going anywhere, our only purpose was to broadcast. Therefore everything had to be subservient to this end. The way of life on Radio Caroline simply clashed with the tradition of the ocean.

She was an elegant 188-foot, 763-ton ship with a 168-foot mast. She had been designed as a passenger Danish ferry, and she still carried that luxurious feeling. We would board the ship on the main deck towards the stern. Either by jumping onboard or by rope ladder up the side. This main deck ran around the outsides of the ship and across in front of the lounge. At the side of the ship, on the main deck, there was a mahogany door that entered into a short passage. Turn left and there was the lounge, a large room surrounded by windows, under which was a cushioned bench. In the middle of the lounge, on the wall facing the front of the ship was a long table bolted to the floor that could comfortably seat twelve people. There was another door on the other side of the lounge that went out onto the deck on the other side of the ship. Then immediately to the right was the door into the galley. Here the Dutch chef created our numerous meals, from simple bacon and eggs to the Dutch delicacy of "rice taffel."

But if as you entered through the mahogany door you turned right and climbed six steps, you then entered through a door to the record library. The walls were lined with LPs and 45s. Straight ahead was the door into the studio, which was surrounded by windows.

On each side of the main deck there were steps leading up to the bridge. The captain's cabin was behind the bridge.

The bow of the ship was a place of winches, chains and ropes, and behind this was our 168-foot mast.

The deck of Radio Caroline

The stern deck was our place for sunbathing, sitting or leaning over the rail, watching the ocean.

As you entered from the main deck, in front were stairs going straight down to the cabins. The cabins were wood paneled rooms containing a bed, a place for clothes and a porthole. The porthole had large bolts, which you closed tight during a storm, otherwise you would be invaded by a drenching wave. At the end of the passage were the showers and toilets.

Beneath the cabins was the engine room that ran the whole length of the under-part of the ship. Here was the main huge engine that was connected by a thick shaft to the propeller. Around it there were metal walkways and platforms for access and repairs. Also there was a separate engine, the electrical generator. Next to this were the transmitters, all twenty thousand watts, with dials, switches, knobs and controls. From the transmitters ran a thick cable through a large insulator to the outside and the mast.

I unpacked and made up my bed in my narrow cabin cell and immediately went up and explored the record library. From the broadcast studio I could hear the number one hit of the day, "Can't Buy Me Love" by the Beatles. Even though I had heard it before, it felt like I had just discovered it.

Since I was going to be doing the morning show, I needed to become familiar with everything available. The suppression of rock and roll by the BBC had isolated me. But now I again had the freedom to listen to what I wanted.

In the ship's music library I found some familiar tunes from my days at the CBC in Canada. There was Buddy Holly's "Peggy Sue," Chuck Berry's "Sweet Little Sixteen," the Coasters' "Yakety Yak" and one of my favorite instrumentals, the Ventures' "Walk Don't Run." But I discovered that a Buddy Holly song, "Not Fade Away," had been recorded by a new British band, the Rolling Stones. This was my kind of music.

When I was living in Yellowknife, one song I used to hear at night coming from some American southern blues station was "Just One Look" by Doris Troy. Now another new British band, the Hollies, had done a version of it. This was the greatest fun that I could ever have imagined. One moving song that I particularly liked was called "5-4-3-2-1." This was from yet another new British band, Manfred Mann. I certainly had a great collection of songs for my radio show.

From the moment I climbed aboard, I had the impression that it was all very proper, very British. Was I the only one who had even heard American rock and roll radio and it's special deejay sound?

Of course, I too had my share of English conditioning. I had been to an English boarding school and had learned proper manners. Perhaps now was the time for me to be polite and just keep quiet.

But being at sea reminded me of the freedom I had once known as a child in the American south. Later in Canada, when I was eighteen, I learned to be independent and self-reliant as a cowboy and ice fisherman. I wanted my radio show to be an expression of my experiences.

When I first went into the studio, I knew I was right to be apprehensive. On-air, the people were not being deejays, but merely announcers. They sat in a booth, while on the other side of a glass window sat an operator who actually played the records. This was the BBC's style of broadcasting and was, in my opinion, completely contrary to being a deejay. With that approach your shows would sound formal, almost as if we were wearing a suit and tie. In fact many of the British radio people did wear ties. This did not fit the free spirit of rock and roll. When you spun or jockeyed your own records, a whole new attitude would emerge. You would naturally be one with the records, with the music, with the jingles, the commercials and your voice.

Uninhibited by the opinions of some operator, you could create an endless array of music, voice and other sounds. There would be life in your radio show that no formal announcer could create.

I wanted to fashion a sound that reminded me of that American fifties radio I loved. That was why I jumped at the chance to join Radio Caroline. There was no way that my radio show was going to be shackled by having to work with an operator. Now was time to throw away our well-behaved, good mannered, English ways.

So I decided to share this with those who were willing to listen. I would encourage them to become true rock and roll deejays as well. I explained all this to the radio staff, pointing out the unique advantages we had on Radio Caroline, where we had a freedom that had never before existed in Great Britain. Let's seize this opportunity, I urged.

Their initial hesitation to doing their shows differently came from not knowing how to operate the equipment. I showed them how easily this could be overcome. In a few hours they were all expert deejays at operating the controls. They were still too mannerly, too polite, but maybe with time this starch would wash out. I hoped so. Then as the weeks rolled by, we all began to discover the fun of this free way of doing radio. And so gradually emerged the sound of Radio Caroline.

That morning I felt at home sitting at the radio console. In front of me were the round knobs and switches of the control panel. On each side was a turntable and above the console there were two cart machines for playing commercials and jingles. A microphone was suspended in the middle and a clock hung on the wall straight ahead, with its long and sweeping second hand.

I cued up a record on the turntable, switched on the microphone and said, "This is Radio Caroline, my name is Tom Lodge and I have some great rock and roll for you. And here's a record that expresses my feeling of being on this wonderful ship, Radio Caroline. Here's the Dave Clark Five with 'Glad All Over.'"

The music thundered from the speakers. I cued up another record, "Just One Look" by the Hollies, and I was off, swaying and bouncing to the music. I was in my glory. And all the while there was the drone of the ship's generator and the gentle roll of the ship moving with the North Sea's slow waves.

Sometimes I was on-the-air for four hours a day and sometimes, when there was a shortage of deejays, I would do more. It didn't matter. I was enjoying every minute. But I never knew if anyone was listening or how many; that's the strange thing about radio, you never know. It is as if I was in my living room playing my favorite records and talking to the wind. But still I loved it.

That very first month, Simon Dee and I took a tape recorder up on the deck of Radio Caroline and recorded the ship's bell. We then used this sound in some of our radio spots. This caught on and soon Ronan as well as everyone else in Caroline House decided to use the bell as our image. So we started to play the bell at the top of the hour. Then it became the Caroline logo on all our documents. The bell was important to us because it gave our radio programs a nautical sound and image. This was also important for the British people because the British have always felt that they are a seafaring people, and this helped connect us to the hearts of the nations. So whenever reporters came on the ship, they wanted a picture of us ringing the bell.

Our schedule on the ship was two weeks on and one week ashore. That was the schedule, though it hardly ever worked out that way since we were short-staffed most of the time. Not to worry, because the two things I loved the most had come together, the sea and music. My first shore leave was a second honeymoon and a glorious reunion with my sons. I also visited with Ronan in some crummy little office in Holborn, a place where our supplies could be organized. We were all little kids who had discovered the greatest, never-ending cookie jar.

And then two things happened. After one month, Ronan moved the whole Radio Caroline operation into a large, opulent mansion in Mayfair, London at 6 Chesterfield Gardens and called it Caroline House. At about the same time, another ship sailed within three miles of us, dropped anchor and started broadcasting. Everything had changed. We had suddenly become grand in Caroline House and we had some competition.

CHAPTER 2

I'm Taking the Top Fifty

Anchored three and a half miles off Felixstowe with our 168-foot mast, we gained immediate attention from both passing ships and people on shore.

Yes, we were strange. We were a new mark on the ocean horizon. The tall mast had an appearance of grandeur, it was a visual statement, but more so, it was a huge audio statement. We were definitely here. Our music blasted through the barricades of the British establishment's music censorship—we were about freedom. At this time there was still concern about rock and roll. Rock and roll seemed to encourage a freedom that was unpredictable, from Elvis' undulating hips to the sexual implications of the beat. Until that Easter Sunday in 1964 when we went on-the-air, Britain had only thirty minutes of pop music a week, from the BBC Light Programme, and evenings of static-filled music broadcasting from Radio Luxembourg, a radio station that played only a one minute taste of each record because it was sponsored by the record companies.

Around this time the transistor radio's price had dropped to a point where many teenagers could afford one. This was a major breakthrough. Cheap transistor radios made it possible for our fans to listen to rock and roll anywhere they wanted—outside their homes and under their bedcovers. I received many letters telling me that they were listening to us secretly, hidden from their parents.

Without the transistor, Radio Caroline might not have happened. Listening on the larger home radios would invite parental scrutiny, and since many parents didn't approve of

In Caroline's office, June 1964

the "noise" we were playing, the number of listeners we had would have been greatly curtailed. Unlike in America, car radios were quite rare and not in demand. Many people relied on public transportation or rode bicycles. Some teenagers used scooters, which became the hallmark of the mods. But Britain had not adopted the American's love of the car. Americans listened to music and made love in their cars while the British were much more under the thumb of the Establishment.

To me, Britain was gray, damp and self-conscious; a place where the right behavior and good manners were more important than having fun. This way of life was ingrained into Brits' proper faces and their solid brick and stone houses. Having just arrived from Canada and America, I was very conscious of the contrast. I was also keenly aware of the pressure of youthful energy trying to burst forth. Radio Caroline was determined to free this energy, and yet, we were just a bunch of young guys playing music and having fun. Ronan was only twenty-four and some were younger. I was the oldest, at twenty-seven, and brought with me the experience of the American pop radio sound and the American deejays' lively approach. I was not part of the radio sound that was familiar to the British ears, the respectable BBC.

As a teenager in England I had been an avid listener to the BBC's Light Programme, especially *The Goon Show*, *Dick Barton—Special Agent*, *The Archers* and the radio dramas. But always the music that was being played on the radio was most unsatisfying. At that time the Musician's Union and the Phonographic Performance Limited group had created a law that only allowed a limited amount of actual records to be played on the only British radio outlet, the BBC. This limitation was called "needle time." Needle time limited how many minutes a day the BBC could actually broadcast with a needle in the groove. To compensate for this limited broadcasting of pop records, the BBC created a small group of classical musicians to play their own arrangements of the current popular songs, either live or to recording tape with the idea that it would be broadcast at a later date. This was particularly boring. Today this must seem most strange, but this is a striking illustration of British culture at the time and their obsessive control of every movement of the loyal British subjects. Before the launch of Radio Caroline, most thought this was a normal way of life.

The only other outlet for records was the scratchy, in and out signal of Radio Luxembourg, which broadcast only at night from the Grand Duchy of Luxembourg. They had such programs as *The Decca Records Show* and *The Capitol Records Show*, which only played one minute of each record. Their only purpose was for these companies to sell their records.

The BBC still found the Beatles acceptable. "I Want to Hold Your Hand," "She Loves You" and "Please Please Me" were considered "safe" music as well as the fact the four were also relatively harmless, with their neat black suits and slightly long but tidy hair.

America and England were more than just thousands of miles apart—they were decades apart in culture. Here are a just a few of the American hits that never happened in England before Radio Caroline: Bobby Vinton's "Mr. Lonely,"

Jan & Dean's "Surf City," Bobby 'Boris' Pickett's "Monster Mash," Sam Cooke's "Another Saturday Night" and just about any other black pop tune.

Underneath this strict societal control, the seeds of a new British culture were beginning to germinate. A few teenagers were getting their hands on both white and black records from visiting American sailors. The teenagers learned how to sing what they heard and played the music with their guitars, drums and keyboards, then performed them at their local clubs. It was this music, the music of the working-class, English teenager that we played on Radio Caroline. There were such groups as the Rolling Stones, the Who, the Yardbirds, the Troggs, the Zombies and many more. We also played the American music of Booker T. & the M.G.'s, B.B. King, Chuck Berry, the Drifters and many artists on the Motown label. In Westminster and Whitehall there was a lot of head-shaking and finger-wagging, but the music was our boss, not the British government. We were for expression and freedom, for life and fun.

These English teenagers got a hold of a few American blues and rock records, and influenced by the music, created a new British rock sound. After this music was exposed and supported by Radio Caroline, it became a part of the British music invasion of America. Like a tidal wave, the American music returned to America with a British flavor. The Yardbirds, the Animals, the Kinks, Led Zeppelin and Van Morrison of Them would never have happened without the help of American sailors and Radio Caroline.

After only a few weeks on-the-air, our radio supremacy

was challenged. I had just finished my show with "Good Golly Miss Molly" by the Swinging Blue Jeans when I looked out the porthole and saw a ship on the horizon. It had a tall mast similar to ours.

I ran up to the bridge. Simon Dee and the captain were looking out to sea with binoculars. "What ship is that?" I asked.

"I'm not sure," said Simon. "But they have a very tall mast."

I motioned to the captain. "How about getting them on the radio and finding out who they are? And what they are doing here next to us?"

He nodded and picked up the radiophone. "This is MV *Fredericia* of Radio Caroline, the captain speaking. Do you read me?"

The speaker boomed loud and clear. "Yes, we read you. This is MV *Mi Amigo* of Radio Atlanta."

I felt a rush in my belly. What the hell's happening? Without a thought, I grabbed the microphone from the captain. "Who's Radio Atlanta? Where are you from?"

"We're from Australia."

"Thanks," I said, stunned. "Okay. Over and out."

We were meant to be the king. We owned the waves. What was another radio ship doing here? And so close, only three miles away. We needed to get Ronan on the line.

Simon was just staring out at the ship. Before we could move, the radio came alive. "This is Ronan. Caroline, do you read me?"

"Yes! This is Tom. Good you called. We were just about to call you."

On Caroline North, 1964

"There is a ship near you. Can you see it?" Ronan said.

"Yes, they say they are MV Mi Amigo of Radio Atlanta from Australia. What's going on?"

"I know."

"Who are these guys and why are they anchoring next to us?"

"Well, Tommy baby, we've got competition. Another radio ship is going to start broadcasting in a few days."

"In a few days!" I said.

"And they're going to be broadcasting only three miles away from us!"

"Three miles!" I shouted. "That's going to confuse everyone." Now I was annoyed.

"It already has confused our advertisers," Ronan replied calmly. "There is a hold on all potential advertising

Ringing Caroline's famous bell

until they can determine which one of us has the largest audience."

"For God's sake, Ronan! We've been on-the-air just a few weeks and we've already got competition from Australia? Who is this Radio Atlanta guy anyway?"

"Cool it, Tommy baby, it's okay. The man's name is Alan Crawford."

"Alan Crawford?" As soon as I said his name I remembered. "Oh, I know, that's the publisher and record company owner." Ronan mentioned his name before about some other ship at Greenore when he was rigging out Radio Caroline. But I had thought no more about it. "What are you going to do now?" I asked.

"I've called for a meeting with Alan Crawford. But for now, you go on with the show. We've got to keep our listeners in the pink. That's all that matters."

"Okay, Ronan, they can't beat our talent!"

Yes, we had the talent. A talented deejay is one who can connect with the audience. Our guys could do that, they loved the music and their enthusiasm was genuine. It made you want to go on listening to them. They knew the right music to play at the right moment. From a distant speaker I could hear our station playing the Dave Clark Five and "Bits And Pieces," reflecting the new tension in the air. It was an unknown, a feeling of uncertainty.

A few days later I was sitting on the stern deck watching an approaching boat. It looked like our tender, which from time to time would bring us supplies. The sun was shining and the sea was calm. Good, I thought, the boat will bring fan mail. I loved the fan mail, the support and the enthusiasm, but above all, the attention from so many young girls. As I watched the boat getting larger, I could hear over our radio speakers Simon Dee introducing "Anyone Who Had a Heart" by Cilla Black. Just then, Jerry Leighton popped his head out the square porthole behind me and said, "Looks like the tender is coming. Maybe there will be some more deejays."

"Looks like Ronan's onboard," I said.

The tender came along side and Ronan jumped across the moving gap and onto our deck. "Okay, you guys," he said. "I don't have much time. We have to talk. We'll meet in the studio so that Simon can be with us."

In the broadcast studio we all crowded around Ronan, wanting to hear the news.

"Well, it's like this," Ronan began. "Alan Crawford and I have made a deal. Radio Atlanta will become Radio Caroline South."

"Have you bought the ship from Alan Crawford?" I asked.

"Oh, goodness no! He'll still owns the ship, but we have made a joint venture for selling advertising, otherwise we still run our own ships. This ship will sail up north and become Radio Caroline North. This way we'll cover the whole of the UK."

"Where will Caroline North be anchored?" asked Jerry.

"That's top secret," Ronan said with a grin. "You'll know when you are almost there. If the government were to find out, they could create problems. But that's not the question. The question is: who is staying on this ship to go up north, and who is going over to the *Mi Amigo* for Caroline South?"

"I'll go over to the *Mi Amigo*," said Simon without any hesitation.

Jerry and I decided to stay on this ship and sail up north.

I liked the ship, and the thought of sailing around the coast, broadcasting as we went, was most appealing.

"Okay," said Ronan. "Jerry, you take over Simon's show and Simon you grab your things and come with me over to the *Mi Amigo*."

"That quick?" said Simon.

"Yes, this is happening now."

"Well, in that case," said Simon, "I'm taking the Top 50 records." Our Top 50 was taken from *Melody Maker*, a British music magazine. The music listed was the music our listeners wanted to hear. The 45s in the Top 50 box were gold to us.

By this point I had worked alongside Simon for three months and we were able to work agreeably side by side

Ronan and Alan Crawford, 1964

and we tolerated each other. But our radio shows were night and day. His presentation was professional but, in my opinion, a little too conventional. I thought his style was a little BBCish. His taste of music was more Doris Day, Frank Ifield and Cliff Richard while I was into the Rolling Stones, Dave Clark Five and Manfred Mann. To have access to such a diversified genre of music was the wonder of Radio Caroline. I was not going to let him have the Top 50.

There is a unique aspect of living in the confined space of a ship that gives people the choice of getting along or living in hell. We chose to get along even though Simon found me a little too uncouth—I think it was my Canadian, backwoods mannerisms.

"No, you are not!" I shouted. My mind was suddenly engulfed with only having Doris Day, Andy Williams, Dean Martin, Perry Como and Rosemary Clooney to play. Horrors! The Top 50 was full of the music that stimulated my very life. The whole idea of being on a ship at sea with no Beatles, no Rolling Stones, no Hollies, no Manfred Man and no Dave Clark Five was the worst nightmare. "No! No! No!" I shouted.

"Damn right, I am!" he said as he moved toward the box of Top 50 records.

I dived for the box, grabbed it first and took off out to the deck.

"I need that!" shouted Simon.

"There'll be plenty of records already on the other ship," I shouted back. "This is our lifeline."

"Okay, enough of this," said Ronan. "We don't have time for this. We have to go, Simon."

Ronan moved quickly and jumped back onto the tender. I scrambled up high, right onto the top of our ship, clutching the box of Top 50. I knew that without these records we would be nothing. Our whole existence was in this small box of 45s, this little box of vinyl. Simon was still shouting at me as he stood on the tender and sailed away. And then, amid the silence, with the sound of the waves sloshing on the side of the ship, Jerry and I looked at each other and began to laugh.

CHAPTER 3

We're Caroline,
the Ship with the Big Mast

Saturday, July 3rd, 1964, was warm and sunny, a classic "let's go to the seaside" day. Many thousands of people were likely to be all along the English coast. I awoke, looked out the porthole and there was the coast of Kent, and then the White Cliffs of Dover. We were on the move. It was 5:30 a.m. and time for me to go on-the-air. I had no idea where we were sailing. The only person who knew was our Dutch captain and he had been given sealed orders. That just added to the excitement. Every moment was an adventure.

I settled into the studio, hit the button on the cartridge tape player and out came "Rinky Dink" by the Johnny Howard Band, my theme tune.

"Good morning to you. This is Tom Lodge with a beautiful Caroline morning and some music for marching around the breakfast table while we sail around the coast of England. Here's a great sound from the Animals with their new release, 'The House of the Rising Sun.'"

Alan Price's organ soared across the airwaves, followed by the voice of Eric Burdon. "There is a house in New Orleans..."

After I had been on-the-air for two hours, Jerry Leighton came down and took over. Since we were the only deejays onboard, we agreed to do two-hour shifts. I went out on deck to stretch. We were approaching Beachy Head and I wanted a closer look. I scanned the shoreline with a pair of binoculars.

"Oh my God!" I shouted. There were crowds of people on Beachy Head. It was completely covered with people. Something was happening on shore. Then it hit me! People had come to see us sail by. I rushed down to the studio.

"Jerry!" I shouted. "There are thousands of people watching us sail by!" I scrambled back up the ladders to the bridge, grabbed a mirror and began reflecting the sun onto the shore. I couldn't have dreamed of this.

Soon it was my turn to go back on-the-air: "Those of you girls on the beach listening to Radio Caroline, take your mirrors out of your purses and reflect the sun at us. Reflect it onto Radio Caroline so that we can see you. You can't miss us, we're the ship with the big, big mast."

It happened in an instant. The coastline lit up with flashing lights. Everything was sparkling. This went on all day, all along the coast. We kept reminding our listeners that we were "the ship with the big, big mast." As the sun gently set down into the west, people began flashing car headlights.

We flashed lights back, kept referring to them on-air and played hits like Lulu's "Shout," the Mojos' "Everything's Alright" and Cilla Black's "You're My World," the current number one on *Melody Maker*'s charts.

That evening our captain, Captain Hangerfelt, came into the studio. We put him on-the-air and, with his strong Dutch accent, he resolved the mystery of our destination. He announced that we were heading for the Isle of Man and were going to drop anchor in Ramsey Bay.

The next morning we were off the north coast of Cornwall and Devon. Again it was a clear, blue, gentle, welcoming sea. It had been dark when we rounded Land's End, but now, with the sun up again, we were ready to draw attention to ourselves.

On-air I said, "It's Sunday morning and I sure miss

Radio Caroline North in the Irish Sea

breakfast in bed and reading the Sunday papers. But in the meantime, here's a moving Chuck Berry song called, 'No Particular Place to Go.'"

Within twenty minutes a speedboat rushed out from the coast, came alongside Caroline and threw a bundle of newspapers onto our deck. The immediate response was exciting. I never experienced such a close connection with the audience.

As we sailed out from the coast of Wales, calmness settled upon us. This coastline was sparsely populated—no lights, boats or mirrors. On-air, I dropped in three or four Welsh words that my mother had taught me. Many years later I met a Welsh farmer who enjoyed hearing my badly pronounced Welsh words. Our ship moved smoothly through the water. There was fullness in the air, a feeling of contentment.

"This is a mellow time," I said. "And here is some music to support this calm feeling. It's the B-side of the record—it should have been the A-side—and I'm dedicating it to all the listeners who can receive us across the mountains of Wales. Here's the Four Seasons and 'Silence is Golden.'"

The seas were calm that night. The moon's light bounced off the sea onto the side of our ship. The night and the music blended into one. We all slept deeply.

The next day we arrived at the Isle of Man. "Hello, Isle of Man," I said on-the-air. "This is Tom Lodge. If you're listening to Radio Caroline, we'd like you to use your mirrors to reflect the sun onto our ship so we can see you! Or if you don't have a mirror handy, flash your car headlights."

Nothing happened. We tried everything. Nothing happened. No response. I asked Jerry, "What's going on? Nobody's responding!"

Jerry was just as mystified.

"Something must be wrong," I said. "Maybe we're not welcome here."

This was strange. We were loved by thousands of people in England. All along the coast we were welcomed with cheers, mirrors and headlights. But now that we had arrived at our destination, the island off which we were planning to spend a long time, there was no response. To not be welcomed by the Isle of Man would be most awkward. This was our new home and we needed their support in order for this battle against the British establishment to work.

Today it may not seem so important, but the music we were playing allowed new musicians and record labels to emerge. It was a David-and-Goliath battle. We needed the support of the people of the Isle of Man.

Looking out the porthole to the Isle of Man

I saw a small boat moving out from the coast. Not a fishing boat or any other boat that we were used to, but a canoe. The two figures in the canoe were rhythmically paddling in our direction. We watched with interest. As they drew near, we could see that it was two men paddling as if they could go on forever.

The canoe came alongside Radio Caroline, one of the men held up an envelope in his right hand. "My wife wouldn't rest until I brought you this," he said.

Jerry reached over the railing and took the envelope. Without another word they canoed back to shore.

I had put a long piece of music on and came down to see what was going on. Jerry opened the letter. From the fold in the page, he took out a piece of heather. He read the note out loud, "Welcome to the Isle of Man."

Tom and Neddy sailing
to the Isle of Man, 1964

Suddenly Jerry laughed. "Oh! That's amazing!" he said. Yes! Now we sure are really welcomed by the people of the Isle of Man. This is it! These people have said yes."

We both waved to the receding men in their canoe and shouted, "Thanks a lot, guys!" The two men waved back and returned to paddling. Maybe this low-key, heartfelt way was more the Celtic response to us. These seemed to be gentle people.

The Isle of Man may have welcomed us, but at the same time things were heating up back in London.

The headline in one newspaper read, "Plan to Seize Pirate Radio." After the autumn election, Anthony Wedgwood-Benn became the Postmaster General and was in charge of the ministry that controlled radio in Britain. One of the first things he did was to go on television and denounce pirate radio: "The pirates are a menace and I don't believe, at all, that the public wouldn't support action to

Tom and Jerry Leighton prepare to ring the bell as Neddy marks time

enforce the law. The pirate radio ships have no future at all. I'm quite convinced of that!"

We were not breaking any laws. Both Radio Caroline South and Radio Caroline North were beyond the three-mile limit, in international waters and outside of the jurisdiction of Great Britain. Both of our ships were away from all shipping lanes and even though we were called "pirates," the Radio Caroline stations were simply offshore radio broadcasting ships.

In fact, the British government recognized us as being outside of their jurisdiction. They treated us as foreigners. When we came ashore, we had to go through customs with our passports.

After the next election cycle, Edward Short took over the Postmaster General position from Wedgwood-Benn. Like Wedgwood-Benn, he also announced on TV his desire to silence us: "I promise legislation that will put all pirate stations off-the-air."

It was a funny game. It was a battle. But the music was flourishing. We were pushing in every direction. We accepted no limit to play and, with our twenty-four hours of rock and roll, there was no end to the party.

In an interview with Nicholas Holmes of the magazine *Weekend and Today*, who sailed out to our "floating jukebox," I explained: "My friends thought I was crazy when I took this job...but I've always gone out on a limb and done crazy things. Sure, I miss female company and the isolation takes some getting used to...but I'm prepared to accept this because I'm getting a kick out of doing something different. Anyway, operating a pirate radio has a nice, audacious British touch about it."

Photo from *Weekend and Today* story, "On the Good Ship Lolly-Pop." Shot after Tom's morning show in an auxiliary booth, the microphone, the ship's dog, "on-air" sign and an ashtray full of cigarette butts are all props. While the magazine is clearly delighted that the "Radio pirates have the politicians in a spin," they still refer to Tom as an "announcer."

Soon our on-air radio crew expanded to include Alan "Neddy" Turner, who had been our radio technician as we sailed north, Tony Jay and Big Jim Murph the Surf. And then, many a listener's favorite, the young fellow from Liverpool, Mike Ahern. Mike and I became close friends.

The deejay needs to be in tune with what's happening now, feel the music he is playing while listening to the relationship between the music, his voice and any other sounds he introduces. The deejay is creating an audio collage that touches the feelings of the listener.

He is always—and only—speaking to one person, even though he may have a million listeners. Radio is an intimate medium, unlike television. The voice is close and can touch you deeply if the deejay is speaking directly from his or her feelings. When radio is working, a listener will feel that the deejay is talking directly to them. This is what we were doing on Radio Caroline North. This was the power of our programming.

One day when the tender came with supplies, fan mail and a batch of newly released records, I received a message from our northern office in Liverpool to go ashore and be the emcee for a Rolling Stones concert in Douglas, the capital of the island nation. Since I loved the Stones, and this would give me a chance to spend a little time with them, I was thrilled.

CHAPTER 4

I'm a Pirate

Iloved to climb the mast and look down. Up there our ship seemed tiny, much too small to support me. Hanging up there, swaying as the ocean moved our ship, I felt like I was flying. But today I had no time to fly, there was a tender waiting to take me ashore. I had a gig. I was going to introduce the Rolling Stones at one of their concerts.

By this time I had been around a little. I had helped open a trendy boutique or supported some new venture or emceed for some up-and-coming group. Later on I even emceed a concert in honor of Princess Margaret, Queen Elizabeth's sister. But now I was going to emcee for the Stones, who had quickly become my favorite group. They just had their first hit single, "It's All Over Now," and I couldn't wait to meet them.

As I climbed down from the mast, Mike Ahern was on-the-air introducing a song that I also played, "Do Wha Diddy Diddy" by Manfred Mann.

Back down in my cabin I stood on my bunk and looked out at the waves through the round porthole with large brass bolts. The sparkling sun reflected on the waves that were shimmering on the mahogany walls and white ceiling.

I turned to my closet and looked through the clothes. What should I wear for my first Rolling Stones concert?

I laid everything out on my narrow 2-foot by 6-foot bunk. I had a collection of cheerful and colorful clothes from a hip, fashionable boutique in Liverpool. Boutiques were springing up everywhere to supply all those who wanted to wear the latest '60s fab fashions. Everything was pretty flamboyant, but I chose a green, satin, full-sleeved shirt with turquoise, tight fitting satin pants, and then my boots, which I had kept from my cowboy days in Canada.

Properly attired, I came on deck feeling the ocean breeze and the warm sun in my face. It felt good to wear clothes with a color and style that matched the spirit of the music.

Tom watches Mike Ahern on the air

The tender dropped me on the dock. It was August 13th, 1964. I found a taxi and climbed in.

The driver recognized me from the newspapers, "You're Tom Lodge, the deejay. I'm a great fan of Radio Caroline. I really like what you guys are doing for rock and roll. All me mates listen to you all the time, between fares, of course. We're great fans!"

"That's great," I said. "We sure are happy to be here off the Isle of Man. Everyone here is so welcoming."

When we arrived at my destination, I pulled out a bill to pay. Before taking it the driver said, "Hey! Could you autograph the money, Tom?"

"Sure." Now that was a new idea, I thought.

I rushed through the stage door and was immediately greeted by Mick, Keith, Brian, Bill, Charlie and a few roadies. Brian Jones came over and took me aside. Together we went over the routine for the evening.

It was hard to ignore Mick Jagger. Sipping a whiskey and Coke, he was pacing back and forth, checking with each person, making sure all was set.

My first impression of the Stones was as a group of young fellows who were not yet swept up in all the hoopla, the glamour and the craziness. Brian was levelheaded. Mick was definitely the businessman of the group. He was probably grounded from his time at the London School of Economics.

They were not yet the Stones that most remember. They all looked so young. Even Keith Richards had a baby-face with no wrinkles at all. Mick, Keith, Brian and Charlie Watts

A pirate with his fan mail

were only around twenty years old, with Bill Wyman being the old man of the group at twenty-seven.

Part of my growing attraction to the Stones was that they were the opposite of the Beatles—no mop-tops, their hair was long and scruffy. They were not wearing matching suits like the Beatles, but different colored shirts and pants. Keith had his shirttail hanging out, something that was totally contrary to the British etiquette, and Mick's shirt was open down to his navel. In fact they were outrageous, not exactly the role models the mothers and fathers of the United Kingdom wished for their children.

Tom warms up
an audience

Mick put out his hand, "So, you're Tom Lodge. Ronan speaks very highly of you."

"Well that's great," I said. "When did you last see Ronan?"

"While we were performing in London last week."

"Where was that?"

"At the Richmond Athletic Ground."

"Did you shake the wickets out of the ground?"

"Yes," Brian interrupted. "We shook their very foundation."

"And so you will tonight," I added.

"You know something," Mick put his face close to mine, looked straight into my eyes and spoke softly, "we intend to sink this island with rock."

"Knock out!" I agreed, patting him on the back.

"And," Charlie said, coming over and putting his hand on my shoulder, "this is going to be our finest concert."

"How is that?"

Charlie laughed, "Because it is the one we're doing."

Bill added from behind, holding up his hands, "The one we're doing is always our finest concert."

"Yes!" we all agreed.

Keith came over and broke the mood. "Hey, there's something wrong with the equipment. I guess we're going to be late going onstage."

"Oh hell," said Brian.

Mick looked a little nervous. "What's happening? How long will it take?"

"We're still working on it," answered one of the roadies.

"But how long will it take?" Bill asked.

"Half an hour, I think."

I could hear clapping from the audience. "We want the Stones! We want the Stones!"

Brian smiled and said calmly, "The audience is getting rather impatient."

Mick turned to one of the roadies, "Hey guys, get it fixed fast!"

I peeped out through the stage curtain. The audience looked restless, the shouting and clapping was getting louder and more insistent.

Keith said, "Hey, we got to do something quick!"

I decided to help. "Okay," I said. "I'll try and calm them down."

Charlie shook his head and laughed, "I wouldn't go out there if I were you. They'll tear you apart!"

"Don't worry," I said. "I'm a pirate!" Now everyone laughed.

I picked up a bunch of incense that was lying on a table backstage. I waved the incense back and forth like a sword, looked back at the group and shouted behind me, "I'll take my chances."

I then lit the whole bunch of incense sticks, held them high like a torch and walked onstage.

Within a few seconds the audience settled into a silence of anticipation. I waved the torch until the flame was blown out, leaving a column of smoke rising from the incense.

The audience waited. I slowly walked around the stage and then, to hold their attention, I passed out the sticks of incense one by one to those closest to the stage. The mood had changed. The audience was calm. We were connecting.

I went to the microphone. "Is Anthony Wedgwood-Benn in the audience? Because if you are, come up here, Anthony! So we can all pelt you with some good fresh tomatoes!"

The audience roared with laughter. Wedgwood-Benn was our nemesis, the government official trying to get Radio Caroline off-the-air.

Thankfully I didn't have to keep it up much longer. From the corner of my eye I could see Bill Wyman signaling me that it was okay to start.

"Okay!" I boomed across the hall. "At last you can all go wild! But first hold your breath! Wait for it! Here they are, the one and only, the greatest group of all time, the Rolling Stones!"

The Rolling Stones burst on stage, bombarding the audience with their new hit, "It's All Over Now." The girls were screaming. The guys were jumping up and down. The beat kept moving, and then without a pause, moved straight into their next song, which was one of the first that Mick and Keith had written, "Tell Me (You're Coming Back)."

The music was solid, powerful, beating deep into our bodies. I danced and watched them from the side of the stage behind the curtain.

Here was a kernel of freedom. Mick's voice opened up the hearts, minds and bodies of a new generation, and gave them permission to let out all their repressed feelings and shatter England's rigid conventions.

At the same time we were out at sea on the airwaves broadcasting fun across the land, we were working hand in hand with the bands that were in the concert halls, together beating down the barricades of repression. The walls erected by the conservative and stuffy English Establishment were tumbling down.

CHAPTER 5

I Can't Explain

The next morning I felt as if I had been steamrolled. I took a taxi from the Chesterhouse Hotel to the pier in Ramsey to catch the tender back to the ship. What a night that had been. The concert was a party, a piece of our everlasting party, a kaleidoscope of endless fun... But that morning the sky was dark, a wind was blowing and beating with squalls of rain. I staggered out to the tender and the skipper, in yellow rain gear, was waving to me. "Come quick!"

I ran the best I could. "What's happening?" I asked.

"There's a storm coming. The report is it's a hurricane. Quick!"

I jumped onto the tender and we headed out to sea. The wind was peeling off the tops of the water, throwing it into our faces. Waves were beginning to build. Our little boat pushed on, bouncing along. Finally alongside the ship, I jumped across the swirling, heaving mass of water to the deck of Caroline. Mike Ahern was waiting.

"It's good you made it," he said. "We're battening down the hatches; we're in for a storm."

I dumped my things on my bunk and headed up to the bridge. Captain Hangerfelt pulled me close, "There's a hurricane warning. We have to pull up anchor and start the engines."

"How bad is it?" I asked.

"We have to head into the wind. Our tall mast could cause us to capsize if we become broadside to the oncoming waves."

"What can I do?"

"Everything must be secured. Any loose objects will be thrown around and broken. Nothing can be left loose."

The ship was hit by a wave. A book and a mug were thrown off the bench and went crashing into the bulkhead.

"That is something else!" I shouted over the wind. "These are sure big waves coming in! I'm going to check out the studio."

Holding onto the rail I pulled myself along the deck to reach the door of the cabin. A wave crashed over the ship. Just in time, I made it through the door. In the studio Mike was taping pennies to the turntable pickup heads to keep them in the groove. Even though the ship was rolling, this extra weight seemed to work. "It's good you're here," Mike said as soon as he saw me. "It's been a long morning, I need a break."

I replaced him at the microphone and waited for the record to end. "That was 'She's Not There' by the Zombies." The microphone was suspended from the ceiling so that it would not pick up the vibrations of the ship's engines. It was swinging back and forth with the roll of the ship. Every time I spoke I had to follow the microphone back and forth. It was strange but I loved it! I was actually having fun.

"Hey," I continued, "we're having some storm here. We are trying to keep the needle in the groove, but bear with us if the rolling ship sends the needle crashing across the record. Just send us good thoughts and we'll keep sending you good music."

I cued up the next record and, as the organ started to play, said, "Here's the song that expresses our feelings... It's Georgie Fame and 'Yeh Yeh.'"

The music moved, the needle stayed in the groove and the ship really rocked and rolled. Within half an hour the storm was full on, waves crashing over the ship. Whenever a wave hit the ship's bow, the bow would plunge deep down into the wave's trough, lifting the ship's stern out of the water, freeing the propellers from the sea's resistance, sending the engines racing with a roar. Each wave was a wall of water. Before each wall was a deep trough into which we fell. It was a roller-coaster ride extraordinaire! The waves would crash right over the bridge. This 763-ton ship was thrown up and down like a toy even though we had 300 tons of concrete in the hold as ballast. The captain was holding us steady into the waves. If we got knocked sideways, we would have capsized. But straight into the wind we went, straight into the waves.

The storm lasted all day and all night. When the rolling

of the ship was too much to keep the needle in the groove, we switched to playing tape. But the music kept going and we took turns being on-the-air. When it was my break, I went down to my cabin to try and get some sleep. This was difficult. I jammed myself in the bunk, but I was rolled and tossed. Eventually I fell asleep. When I woke, I had no idea where I was or how long I had been asleep. The storm was over and the sun was shining through the porthole as though nothing had happened. My cabin was a different story. It was definitely time to clean up.

I had almost finished when Mike came down. "Hey Tom, there's a whole pile of new releases that we haven't looked through yet. Have we got some time to do that now?"

"Sure," I replied, and up we went to the lounge.

Despite the government's efforts to shut us down, for some reason they could not stop the record companies from sending us their records. Every week we would receive hundreds of LPs and 45s. The record companies would deliver the records to Caroline House on Chesterfield Gardens in Mayfair, London, and our staff would ship them out to us on the next supply tender along with our supplies of food and fuel. But it seemed that for every diamond record there was a lot of dirt. If we were lucky, five percent would be any good. It used to amaze me how much poor music was released, yet looking back, it was one of the most prolific periods of high quality music.

One morning up on deck I saw Jerry throw a 45 into the ocean. It flew like a Frisbee across the blue sky before landing on a sunlit wave. Record-throwing was the favorite sport on Caroline. Most times the discs would sail through the air a few feet above the water. Sometimes they would skim the ocean like large, black pebbles.

"Here, let me have some," I said, grabbing a pile of 45s. I looked at the label of the 45 on top: The Who, "I Can't Explain." "Hey, you can't throw this one away."

Jerry glanced down. "Which one is that?"

"This is that new group, the Who."

"Let me see. Oh, that's trash."

"No, Jerry, I like this one." I looked at the label again. "Yeah, I want to play this on my next show."

"Be my guest. Everyone else thinks its trash. I mean, it's just a bunch of noise."

"Good noise!" I said. "Good noise. It's got great energy. It's got that let-it-all-hang-out feeling. I'm tired of all this 'nicey-nicey' music. The drummer is new, refreshing, solid, and I love that raw guitar sound. The singer has a good sounding voice and there is something unique about the bass player, he is not just doing your usual boom, boom, boom."

My explanation wasn't having much effect. I put the record aside. "Yes, I like this one. I guess I'm a rebel at heart."

By the end of April 1965, "I Can't Explain" reached number 8 on the charts.

We flipped a few more records into the sea before heading up to the lounge to meet Mike. On the table in the lounge were piles of records. I took a record and placed it on the turntable.

"That was a good one!" Neddy said. Everyone agreed and I put it in the "yes" pile.

I played another record.

"Naw!" was the general response and I put it in the "no" pile.

And on it went, with most records going into the "no" pile, a few into the "yes" pile and some into the "maybe" pile. We also each had our own favorite piles, our personal choices. This ritual was carried out whenever new records came onboard.

It was the beginning of 1965 when "Tired of Waiting for You" by the Kinks, "The Last Time" by the Rolling Stones, "Don't Let Me Be Misunderstood" by the Animals and "It's Not Unusual" by Tom Jones arrived onboard. We were all unanimous that these should go in the "yes" pile. If it hadn't been for the offshore radio stations, many of these records and many of these artists would never have been heard. Jay Thomas on *Ed Sullivan's Rock 'n' Roll Classics* said: "In the summer of 1965 the release of his [Tom Jones'] first single 'Its Not

Another sport on Caroline was skipping records off the water

Unusual' was considered too hot for BBC radio. So, a pirate radio station called Radio Caroline broke the song in Britain."

Later that summer another record by the Who appeared and I still stood alone with my opinion.

"I like it," I said.

"How could you like that?" asked Mike.

"Anyway, Anyhow, Anywhere," said Neddy, reading the label. "No way, not now, not here. Huh! And they're called Who. Weird name."

"Okay, you guys, I like it. I'm going to play it on my morning show," I insisted.

Like the rest of the guys, I also made a few mistakes. I turned down P.J. Proby with "Hold Me," which reached #2. I did not like Brian Poole & the Tremeloes' "Someone Someone," which also reached #2. I also didn't like the Shadows, the Bachelors and the Fourmost, which made me shudder. But then I also wasn't a big fan of "She Loves You" and "I Want to Hold Your Hand." They were what I called "teeny-bopper" music. In fact, it was not until the Beatles' "Can't Buy Me Love," a number that came out just before we went on-the-air, that I began to enjoy their music. Despite the hits and misses, there was always plenty of great music to play. Everyday I was excited to sit down at the microphone and turntables and play the latest offerings.

Sorting the new records was always a fun time for us, and when we finished someone would say, "Hey, how about another beer?" and then we would break out in crazy antics. One of the guys would run down to the shower room and come back with shaving cream and start spraying us with it. We would run out onto the deck and the chase was on. Someone would climb the mast or grab a rope and swing down from an upper deck. And when the night came, we would walk around the deck holding fluorescent tubes high in the air and, because of the strong radio frequency generated from our mast, the tube would light up. We looked like Jedi warriors in this pre-Star Wars era.

A few weeks later I had just returned from my week's leave onshore and I greeted Mike from the tender. "Guess what, Mike? I just heard that the Who's song, 'Anyway, Anyhow, Anywhere,' has reached number twelve. Great, eh?"

"No accounting for bad taste, you know."

Around this time I also started receiving a lot of fan mail, a lot of it thanking me for playing the Who. It seemed that our audience loved their music. They were also building a loyal following in the clubs and the venues.

As I walked into the lounge, Jerry and Neddy greeted me. "What's the gossip?" I asked.

"Well it's like this, these two seagulls have been having an affair and we are all terribly shocked." We all laughed. "But besides that," Neddy continued, "the only mishap is there ain't no girls here."

Jerry winked at me. "I guess you solved that problem while you were ashore."

"That's for me to know and you to guess."

"Hey," Mike said. "Tell us. At least you can make us jealous."

"But here's the good news," I said. "We now have eight million listeners. Ronan had a poll taken and we are sailing high."

THEY SAID IT COULDN'T BE DONE

From an in-house magazine, *Exclusive Radio Caroline and its Stars*, 1965

"Great! So we shall keep playing then, we are something special," said Neddy.

I nodded in agreement. "But you want to hear a funny story?"

"Sure," said Jerry.

"Well, this little government guy came into Caroline House with a writ for Radio Caroline. He wanted to serve the company. But he was totally confused when he discovered that there is no such company as Radio Caroline because we are run by four different companies and none of them are called Radio Caroline. They are all registered in different parts of the world and each company is owned by other companies, also registered in different parts of the world."

"Wow!" Mike shook his head. "That is a lawyer's nightmare."

"Ronan is pretty smart," said Neddy.

"So what happened?" asked Jerry.

"He left. And that was that."

We laughed, sat in the lounge and had a beer.

CHAPTER 6

Wigan Pier Oil Well

I loved our battle with the British establishment. It made me feel alive and gave my life even more purpose. But I was lucky. Even though I was a married man I had the full support of my family. Jeanine was totally behind me. She never had many problems with the rebellious life I had chosen.

We met in London and then a year later, in 1957, we got married in Paris. The birth of my first son, Tommy, occurred when I was working for the Canadian Broadcasting Corporation in Yellowknife, Northwest Territories, Canada. My second son, Brodie, was born in Hampstead, London. Lionel, my third son, was born in the Highlands of Scotland. I guess our traveling lifestyle made it easy for us when I set out to sea to join Radio Caroline. Even though my three boys had no choice in our traveling ways, it has given them a worldly view, allowing them to see life more objectively. This has given them an advantage over those who have only known one home. They have an independent, philosophical spirit. Most people I know are attached to stability and conformity, where security is important. This seems to limit their creativity and ability to discover, often resulting in them missing out on the rewards life gives you when you step out of the familiar.

My family finances were somewhat sparse, but now, at last, we were covering our expenses. In fact during those three years on Caroline I had done well enough to buy a house in the Cotswolds, Gloucestershire. It was a place where my wife and my sons could be close to my mother and it was also near where I had lived as a boy. My brief times ashore were often taken up with concerts and guest appearances, for which Jeanine and the boys gave me much encouragement. In fact it was Jeanine, under the name of Romy, who started my fan club and kept it running to the end. She didn't use her real name because we wanted to make the fan club appear separate from us. With the name Romy, she was a fan, not my wife.

After two weeks on the ship—sometimes longer—it was always a treat to go ashore. I was so used to the continual moving and rolling of the ship that standing on solid ground was most strange. It felt heavy on the feet and the legs; it was as if the ground was pushing back at me. There was nothing with which to roll the body. It would take a few hours for me to get used to walking on a surface that did not move. It also took a bit to acclimate myself to the invading crash of so many people, so many strangers and so much noise. But soon I was more than ready to dive into this world of life, movement and surprises.

I was always thrilled to return to the warmth of my wife and three sons. From the Isle of Man I would fly to London. Once there I would pick up my white Triumph Spitfire convertible, equipped with Italian air horns, and take the A40 highway to Gloucestershire. At that time there was no speed limit outside of the built up areas, so I would drive at 90 mph. It was exhilarating to wind my way through the country and up into the hills of the Gloucestershire Cotswolds.

Our stone house sat high on a hill overlooking the village of Thrupp. The house had been named "Spion Kop," after a battle in 1900 during the Boer War. I changed it to "Brandon," a name of more elegance.

As I wound around and up the narrow limestone-walled roads near our home, I would turn on my loud Italian air horns, which would play a series of four notes over and over again. Pretending the air horns were the bugles of old, welcoming the king back to his castle, I was hoping that my boys would hear me and come running. The sound would echo through the hills in a cascading return of jubilation. At the house Jeanine and my three boys did come running, and we cascaded into a delightful tangle of hugs.

I would return with gifts, records and stories. Jeanine would have a king's meal ready, as only the French can create. Our brief times together were always special. We would take drives or visit our friends Lynn and Eva Chadwick at Lypiatt Park. During our visits with Lynn and Eva we would enjoy Lynn's latest sculptures, spend time with their son Simon and play with their other children, Sarah,

Sophie and baby Daniel. Lynn was becoming one of England's most celebrated sculptors, with his home evolving into a mecca of celebrity parties.

Jeanine had a boutique in Stroud named Sure Shot. On Caroline whenever we found a newly-released record that we believed would be a hit, we called it a sure shot. She would

Left, Dutch cook on Radio Caroline North
Below, Caroline North dining room

design clothes for the boutique and this was our way of bringing the life of the '60s to Stroud. Her clothes were always a hit.

My visits home were a time of romance and fun. Sometimes my breaks were cut short, if I had to emcee a rock concert or put in an appearance at some swinging sixties event. But still these days were a whirl of color, laughter and a feeling of endless sunshine.

Back on Caroline the feelings continued. But on one of those calm, sunshine-filled mornings at sea I accidentally insulted my audience. I was doing my morning show, really enjoying myself, playing lively music, the kind that moved, the stuff you want to wake up to. I had come into the studio just before 6 a.m. with an armful of LPs, 45s and a handful of fan mail. I had checked out the boxes of 45s that were laying around the mixing console to make sure that everything I wanted to play was on hand. My first number was "Woolly Bully" by Sam the Sham and the Pharaohs. After the song finished I gave my horn two honks, greeted our listeners and played "We Gotta Get out of This Place." This was a new release from the Animals and a song I was longing to play on-the-air. I followed it with the Yardbirds' "Heart Full of Soul" and my favorite, "Anyway, Anyhow, Anywhere" by the Who. I was jumping, the ship was rolling and I hoped the listeners were enjoying the party.

It was time to read some fan mail. I picked a letter that was covered with drawings of hearts and lipstick kisses. After the Who song, I read the letter aloud:

Dear Tom,
I love your show. I listen all the time. I love all you guys

out there. Thanks for the music. It's great having Caroline.
Would you please play a request for Wigan Pier?
Love, Vye

"Wigan Pier?" I said. "You have to be joking, Vye! How can there be a Wigan Pier? Wigan is inland and piers are on the ocean. But I'll play a song especially for you. Here are the Fortunes with 'You Got Your Troubles.'"

And that was how the drama began. When the tender arrived with the next batch of fan mail I was literally swamped with letters asking questions like, "How could you be so rude to our Wigan Pier?" and "Don't you know that Wigan Pier is famous?" Every two weeks when the tender dropped off supplies I kept getting letters about Wigan Pier. Finally I got a letter that explained the story. George Formby was one of Britain's favorite singers/entertainers from the middle of the twentieth century. His father was also an entertainer and performed at the many seaside holiday piers around the coast. His father used to say, "I've entertained at every pier in this country, including Wigan Pier." Wigan was his home but it had no seaside pier, it was inland. That was the joke. But Wigan Pier and the memories were in the hearts of the people of Lancashire. Now I was the joker. I had ridiculed something special. I had touched a nerve.

After I returned from a two-week shore leave, I was back on-the-air playing "Help" by the Beatles. As the record was ending I made my apology:

"It's good to be back on Caroline. And guess what? I've been to Wigan and I found the pier. Yes, the famous George Formby Wigan Pier. I sure put my foot in my mouth. There *is* a Wigan Pier. There's no seaside there, there's no place to sing, but I've found something else. I was standing on the dock of the old canal, it's hardly a pier, but there I was standing and looking in the water and all I could see was dirty, oily water. Yes, dirty old oil! 'Ha!' I said. 'There has to be oil here! You know, the good stuff, black gold!' I started digging and sure enough, I discovered oil and formed the Wigan Pier Oil Well Company and you can be a shareholder in this great oil discovery by simply sending a self-addressed, stamped envelope. As a shareholder you'll receive a share by return."

I gave my rubber ball horn a honk and put on the Byrds and their cover of Dylan's "All I Really Want to Do."

Three days later I was swamped again with mail. I had sacks of envelopes coming in and sacks of shares going out. Each share had some crazy picture of me and these words:

This is to cert and fly that the bare her is a share grabber in my theatrical, non-existent Tom Lodge Wigan Pier Oil Well whose out of his bird Press and Dent can be heard Dawn Busting 6 to 9 am on Caroline 199 giving mourn ewes of this great fiasco.

And yes, my "great fiasco" was a huge success.

New music kept coming from the bands and groups onshore, and we kept playing their songs. This was a continuous flow of music coming to us and then being broadcast back to the increasing millions of listeners.

Many new record labels were forming, making it easier and easier for musicians to be recorded and then, through us, to be heard. Before we came on-the-air there had only been four record companies. Now every week a new record

Tom as emcee with
Princess Margaret
in attendence

label emerged. Many of the bands themselves were forming
their own label.

I continued riding this wave of energy and exuberance.
I had that feeling you get when you first learned to ride a bi-
cycle or roller-skate or swim. It seemed as if I could not get
enough. Everyday I was wanting more and more. By way
of the mail and our public appearances we were connecting
with these friendly, welcoming northern folk. I was enjoying the trips ashore, opening a boutique in Blackpool, doing
gigs in Liverpool. Liverpool put me close to the birthplace
of the Beatles and many other groups. I liked exploring the
local scene.

On one trip I dropped into Radio Caroline's northern office and they asked me if I would emcee a gig at the Center 63 Club on my next shore leave. "Princess Margaret will be there," I was told.

The event was for some local charity. A little Royal patronage would always encourage people to contribute. And I guess my appearance also had a beneficial effect. But my main interest in doing this gig, or any other, was to meet our listeners, to find out which of the songs we were playing were of most interest. It was important to feel the feedback from Radio Caroline supporters. There was a side benefit, too. They would always put me up in a comfortable hotel.

I guess I have never been too impressed with royalty. When I was on stage, Princess Margaret sat only ten feet away but I never spoke with her. I guess I was too eager to mingle with the crowds.

I was on top and feeling good. I was preparing to get back to the ship when I got a call from Ronan. I should finish packing my bags and instead head south. He refused to tell me why over the phone.

CHAPTER 7

A Kaleidoscope of Colors

On the plane to London I was seated in the back. As I waited for takeoff I heard a lot of noise at the front of the plane. I looked up and there was a young fellow with sharp brown eyes. His hair was flying about in all directions as he danced in the entrance. It was the Who's drummer, Keith Moon. I recognized him from the publicity photos that came with the records. Keith never stopped to speak to anyone. He placed his luggage above his seat and then went up and down the aisle drumming on everybody's seat. The passengers smiled and some joined in with the merrymaking. Keith had a certain charm that relaxed people, plus an extraordinary sense of rhythm, so nobody thought there was anything chaotic in his actions.

At first, his band mates Pete Townshend, Roger Daltrey

and John Entwistle, sat quietly in their seats paying Keith little attention. But soon they were chatting with some passengers across the aisle. I went over to them and, standing by their seats, I said, "Hello, Pete. Hello, Roger, John. I'm Tom Lodge. I'm a deejay on Radio Caroline."

"Oh, sure. I know you," said Pete. "We were just listening to you in Liverpool."

I nodded. "I've been playing your records since 'I Can't Explain' and 'Anyway, Anyhow, Anywhere' came out."

Roger brightened up, "Good on you. We love the exposure."

"Yeah, 'Anyway, Anyhow, Anywhere' is what we on Radio Caroline are all about. It just says it. It says, I can go anywhere I choose, that's our very way of life."

"You know," said John, "when you guys sailed around the coast broadcasting, we knew that the music world had changed."

"And," added Pete, "that opened all the doors."

"John," I said, "on 'I Can't Explain,' you play a mean bass line. I love the way you actually play the bass and don't just strum do, do, do, da, da, da, like most people do."

"Thanks, that's because I see the bass as a musical instrument and not just for rhythm."

Pete chimed up, "That's because we think that rock and roll is more than just music for kids."

"Yeah," agreed Roger, "it's much more."

"You know," added Pete, "rock and roll is a fantastic release in this crazy world. I think it's important."

"For sure," I agreed.

Then Keith came bouncing down the isle and started to

drum on my head. They all laughed. He sat down in his seat, took a swig of his drink and closed his eyes.

We spoke a little longer and then I went back to my seat. Even though I was a great fan of theirs, at that time they were not yet stars. England was bursting at the seams with new bands all trying to push through to prominence, all vying for attention, and the wonder was so many of them did have a lot of talent.

Once I landed in London I decided to make a small stop before heading to Caroline House. I had been reading about the London fashion boutiques in the music magazines and now was a good chance to check them out. They said that this was where all the bands' colorful clothes were being created and everyone who was with it shopped there.

I climbed up the stairs from the Piccadilly Underground station and stopped. Right in front of me, in the middle of the Piccadilly roundabout, was a statue of Eros, the primordial God of lust, beauty, love and intercourse, standing on one foot on top of a fountain with his wings spread wide. "Wow," I said to myself, "that's our God beckoning us to have fun and live."

I walked along Glasshouse Street through Golden Square. Everywhere I looked there was something new. I had never felt this in London before. The once dark, damp houses now seemed to shine. Had people been painting their front doors? Were the streets cleaner? Was there more sunshine? Even the trees and plants along the road and in the square seemed vibrant. It was like the light green leaves of spring after a long winter.

I kept walking and turned into the narrow Carnaby Street, with its three story buildings that had been converted into boutiques. It was only three blocks long and crowded with young people chatting and smiling. Everywhere you looked there was an incredible array of colorful clothes both on the street and displayed in the boutiques' windows. There was John Stephen's His Clothes, I Was Lord Kitchener's Valet, Mr. Fish, Kleptomania, Mates, Ravel and much more. It was a sensual thrill, a kaleidoscope right there on the street. I felt like I could fly, soar and glide with ease.

I entered the John Stephen's boutique and was engulfed by the seductive aroma of incense. I saw Lance Percival, an actor, comedian and impersonator trying on clothes in front of a full-length mirror. The previous year he had done the voice of Paul McCartney and Ringo Starr in a cartoon series called *The Beatles*, which had been a television success. I introduced myself and we chatted about Radio Caroline while Mr. Stephen and his assistant, a young, attractive girl in a tight miniskirt with red net tights brought us clothes to try on.

Mr. Stephen, who was dressed in an Edwardian high buttoned suit and a pink ruffled shirt, held out a flamboyant, gold braided jacket and said to Lance, "How about this one?"

"Anything for a giggle," said Lance with his hands on his hips. He took the jacket, put it on and examined himself in the mirror.

Yes! Anything for a giggle, I thought to myself. Life was becoming the most delightful giggle.

I purchased three sensational outfits from different boutiques then hailed a taxi to Caroline House.

"6 Chesterfield Gardens," I said as I climbed in.

The cab driver looked over his shoulder. "Okay mate, you going to Radio Caroline's place?"

"Yes, please."

"That's a really great radio station; I love the courage of those boys. Are you with them?"

"I'm on Caroline North."

"Oh yeah, I can't get that one.

"No, we broadcast off the Isle of Man," I said.

"Well there you go then, too far away. What's your name?"

"Tom Lodge."

"Hey, I know who you are. You were on at the start and

The entrance to
Radio Caroline in
the heart of Mayfair

then you sailed away. That was something, you guys sailing around the coast with thousands of people following you and flashing their lights at you. Yeah, I remember that."

Soon we arrived at Caroline House. "I'd like you to give me an autograph for my girl; she's crazy about Radio Caroline. Her name is Vicky."

"No problem," I replied.

Caroline House was a palatial 4-story palace at 6 Chesterfield Gardens. The entrance had four pillars, with a large door opening into a tiled vestibule. To the right were the offices of the reception, secretaries and accounting. Down the passage was the elevator and behind that was a recording production studio.

As you entered, straight ahead was a wide curving, blue carpeted staircase leading up to a wide hardwood floor open passage. To the front was Ronan's office, to the back were the advertising offices. Ronan's office ran the full front length of the building, with floor to ceiling windows. Across the wall, at right angles to the front, was a blown-up photograph of Radio Caroline North.

Also on this floor were the offices of other Radio Caroline executives. On the next two floors were offices of other people in the music business, including Kit Lambert, the Who's manager.

The basement was where the mail was sorted and then prepared for delivery to both ships. Bags and bags of fan mail would arrive and were almost continually sorted for delivery to the deejays.

The location of Caroline House was ideal for business.

It was in the heart of London's Mayfair, the hub of advertising and Britain's most prestigious corporations. Chesterfield Gardens was a cul de sac off Curzon Street, two blocks from Park Lane and Hyde Park. Here was the center of the buzz of the West End, the entertainment world and the music business. Oxford Street, Piccadilly Circus and Carnaby Street were close by. And Radio Caroline was the center.

I loved coming to Caroline House, walking into this mansion and taking the carpeted grand staircase two steps at a time. The place was always abuzz with smiling, enthusiastic, young people. There were music people wanting their records played, fans wanting a piece of the energy and tourists from Europe and America. Walking into Caroline House was like swimming in a sea of endorphins and happening dreams and aspirations.

This time instead of bouncing up the stairs, I decided to take the elevator. Two other people squeezed in with me. I recognized one of them. Eric Burdon of the Animals. "Hi Eric, I'm Tom Lodge."

He smiled and we shook hands. And then to my surprise he pulled a six-gun out of his satchel, a revolver. It was shiny, strangely real and strictly illegal in England. He looked at me with a gleam in his eyes. "I just got this. Isn't it beautiful."

"Yes, it is," I said with surprise. "But what for?"

"Oh, I just love guns. And this is a real cowboy gun."

"Well, Eric," I said, "I give up."

The elevator door opened on the second floor. I said good bye and headed straight for Ronan's office. I sat down in one of the chairs in front of his desk, waiting for him to finish his phone call. Ronan's office was a large room on the first floor overlooking Chesterfield Gardens in Mayfair, London. One wall was wallpapered with a huge photograph of Radio Caroline North, making the ship the idol of our work. On the adjacent wall there were two large, floor-to-ceiling windows, which gave the room a feeling of royalty. Next to Ronan, on his desk, was a bust of John F. Kennedy. I was pleased to see the bust; we all had so much love for JFK and were devastated by his death. Besides, it made perfect sense for Ronan to have the bust there, from one Irishman to another.

"Of course you can't, Mr. Short," said Ronan. Edward Short was then the assistant to Anthony Wedgwood-Benn, the Postmaster General, who was in charge of British radio.

"I understand you perfectly. But I assure you, Mr. Short, we are not doing anything illegal. All of our broadcasting will stay in international waters. We are like the birds, flying freely across the ocean. By the way, can I interest you in a free ocean holiday in the North Sea? No. Oh well, that's too bad then. Goodbye, Mr. Short."

Ronan hung up. "I love speaking with these government officials. They are so locked in with no fun. Poor fellows."

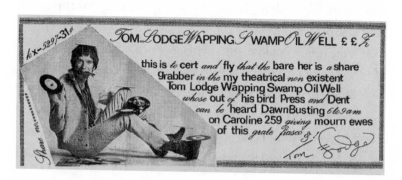

We both laughed and I asked him why he had me flown down.

"Well, it's like this," he said, "while you've been up north, another broadcast ship arrived from Texas, Radio London."

"Yes, I know," I said. "They have those American radio singing jingles and they are using the Drake Format, the typical American Top Forty radio format sound. Yes, powerful stuff."

"There was a recent radio survey that wasn't good. Apparently Radio London has ten listeners to Caroline South's one. Alan Crawford's programming was too conservative, it didn't have the punch. So all of Caroline South's advertisers switched to Radio London and Alan Crawford went broke. So I ended up buying Caroline South."

"Wow! That's fantastic. I love it!" I said.

"Here's where you come in," continued Ronan, leaning forward and touching my arm. "You have created a sound and programming on the North ship that really is the expression of Radio Caroline, an expression that we are all about."

"Thank you, Ronan, I like that sound, too."

"Now," Ronan looked directly at me, "I want you to take over the programming and get our audience back from Radio London. I want you to introduce the programming that you are using on the North Ship and bring that programming to the South ship."

"Good, I can do that," I said enthusiastically. "But I'll need two things: a whole new radio staff and free control of the music."

"Why do you need new deejays?"

"Because the ones that are there have a vested interest in the old programming and will resist change. I need to start from scratch. I need young, youthful guys who love the current music scene, who have a positive outlook and are adventurers. I need to create a new and different kind of radio programming in order to beat the Drake Format. I need to create a fun, high-spirited ship."

"Sounds like fun," Ronan said. "Okay, that's good. Start collecting your deejays. Talk to Frances, she'll give you a hand. Don't forget to have fun too, Tommy.

In England when Radio Caroline went on-the-air, the British radio dials were labeled in meters, that is the length of the radio wave measured in meters. But in the US the radio dials are labeled in frequencies in kilohertz (kHz), which is how frequently the peak of the wave passes by.

Radio Caroline went on-the-air at 199 meters on the English radio dial, which is about 1500 kHz on the American AM radio dial. This was the ship that sailed up north to the Isle of Man and became Radio Caroline North. "Radio Caroline on One Nine Nine."

Radio Atlanta, which became Radio Caroline South, was originally broadcasting on 201 meters, but on April 18th 1966 changed to 259 meters on the English radio dial, which is about 1150 kHz on the American radio dial. "Radio Caroline on Two Five Nine."

Caroline South was playing a type of easygoing music known as "middle of the road" programming. Music by Andy Williams, Perry Como, Frankie Vaughan and Brenda Lee was often played on Caroline South whereas Caroline

North played the McCoys, the Rolling Stones, Bob Dylan, Sonny & Cher and Wilson Pickett. It was this more youthful, rebellious sound and lifestyle that I would need to bring to Caroline South if I was to get the audience back from Radio London. Though Radio London's Drake Format was a successful, American-proven radio format, it was still an automatic system. It still had the deejays locked into a routine. Not as tightly controlled as the BBC, but still restricted. I believed that restraint-free music would always outshine any automatic system.

Over the next couple of weeks, I interviewed many people and slowly put a team together. When we eventually arrived onboard, we were a close team of deejays yet totally different. Each show had its own unique character. I encouraged the deejays to be themselves on-the-air, to allow their personalities to be a part of the show. I had chosen them, out of many applicants, because they had a flavor that would translate through the medium of radio, a way to connect with the audience and keep them listening.

There was Keith Hampshire, a light-hearted, easygoing and tall twenty-year-old from Canada. He brought with him that American, happy sound. There was nothing in life that he could not turn into a positive. Keith knew how to keep the show moving. He understood the collage nature of a deejay show, where the voice, the music, the commercials and the jingles are all materials for a continual flowing sound. He was also a singer with an attractive tenor voice and would eventually become a pop star. The other deejays on our team were Mike Ahern, Dave Lee Travis, Emperor Rosko, Robbie Dale, Graham Webb and Tony Blackburn.

Mike Ahern, who came down from the North ship, had a slight Liverpool accent and a twinkle in his eyes that made you feel warm in your belly. He never said too much and left you wanting more.

Dave Lee Travis was a good-spirited and good-looking twenty-one-year-old who called himself DLT on-the-air. He was a middle-class Derbyshire Englishman with a goatee. His touch of northern accent gave a tilt to his presentations and a hint at humor. He was tall and solid, and it showed on his radio shows.

Our North American deejay was Emperor Rosko, the son of the Hollywood producer Joe Pasternak. He was a forceful guy who brought the flowing patter and personal jabs of the 1950s with him. But then to spice it up, he always had perched by his microphone his myna bird, who chirped in at the most unexpected times with, "You're wrong!," "Not today!" or "Look out, Rosko!" This unexpected chatter always kept Rosko on a funny edge, but best of all was the bird's way of whistling as if he had seen a beautiful girl pass by. This gave Rosko a chance to build on the fiction that there was some girl onboard, at least until the bird would butt in and say, "Not today!"

Robbie Dale was twenty-six and a high-energy fellow by the way of Littleborough, Lancashire. He had that special, deep "radio" voice and he knew how to use it, mixing it in with the records and weaving it through his shows. He loved all the different kinds of music that were flying around the charts, from Sandy Shaw with "Long Live Love" to the Rolling Stones' "Get Off My Cloud."

Twenty-two and imported straight from Australia with

that strange humor, Graham Webb was our "Aussie." His Australian accent brought a touch of the unexpected to the English ear. It was a touch of the wild. He loved rock and roll and was always looking for the crazy side of life. This always made his shows fresh and entertaining.

Tony Blackburn was the love of all the mothers. He was from Guilford Surrey and was easy going with that Beatles-look marked by his mop top haircut. On-the-air he was warm and friendly. Tony made you feel safe and cuddly. He knew how to lull you into the next song. Like Keith, he too was a singer, but would never have a hit. Our team was complete with strong man Rick Dane and the lively Tommy Vance.

Then there was me with my mixture of English and Canadian accents. I was influenced by the American deejays yet had listened to BBC radio growing up. I had emerged out of the wilds of Canada as a cowboy and Arctic fisherman. I was raised by a poet father and painter mother but had a famous pro-establishment grandfather, Sir Oliver Lodge, who made the first radio broadcast in 1894 at Oxford University during the feature presentation at the British Association for the Advancement of Science's annual conference.

Thus, Sir Oliver became the first person to make a public demonstration of radio broadcasting and is now recognized by the Royal Society, who placed a plaque at Oxford University's museum lecture room to commemorate this breakthrough in communications. This demonstration was made two years before Marconi's first radio broadcast in 1896. My grandfather also invented the loud speaker, the vacuum tube (valve), the variable tuner, the spark-plug and many other inventions still of value today. And here I was, his grandson, sailing high on the transmission waves of radio.

My shows were punctuated with honks from my rubber bulb car horn. I would talk over the music intros and use sound effects between my words to enhance the rhythm of the show.

When all was ready, a few of us arrived at the *Mi Amigo*, Radio Caroline South. She was a roughly 98-foot long, 129-ton ship with a 141-foot mast. She was designed to be a cargo ship and sat low in the water. There was little luxury with the *Mi Amigo*. The bridge was high at the stern of the ship, with the mast at the bow. On the main deck from bow to stern, there were five rooms in succession. First the transmitter room, then the lounge, then the galley and behind that the record library leading into the broadcast studio.

Down below, almost at sea level, were the cramped cabins and further below that was the engine room and transmitter room.

This was a sailor's ship. To live on this ship you needed to love the sea. Being relatively small, the *Mi Amigo* reacted to every wave.

Once onboard I called the current deejays together and said, "Okay fellows, there is going to be a change of deejays."

"What do you mean?" one asked.

"Well, it's like this," I explained. "You are all to go to Caroline House and see Ronan. There has been a change of plans. Ronan will bring you all up to date. Some of you are going up to Caroline North. But I don't have the details. You are all to pack your bags and catch the waiting tender to shore and take the train to London. That's all I know."

"Who's going to do the shows?" someone asked.

"These guys who have just come onboard," I said.

"Okay," another one said with a smile on his face, "let's go ashore and paint the town red."

That was how Radio Caroline South went from easy listening to rock 'n' roll. This new team was enthusiastic, fired up and ready to go.

"Here's the situation," I said at one of the early meetings. "We have to get the audience back from Radio London. That's it! That's our mission."

"They have a great sound," Dave said. "Are we going to use the same format, the Drake Format?"

In Caroline's Studio

"No, we would never beat them that way. Here's the deal. We're going to use a new formula. A formula that I know will bring the audience back from Radio London. This has never been done before on any radio station. We're going to pioneer a new system. Here it is. First, the deejay is not allowed to prepare his show in advance."

"Yeah?" Robbie's head shot up. "Wow! How does this work then?"

"You get all the records and albums that you might want to play on your show and place them around you in the studio at the console. There'll be a box for the Top 40, a box for the new releases, a box for our favorites and a fourth box for the goldies, the old hits."

"Then what?" asked Rosko.

"Now, here's the important part. You can only decide what to play when the one before is playing. There is no preparation."

"That could be a bit dicey," Mike said.

I needed to convince them right away. "You've got to feel your show. Not think about it. You've gotta be right in it. You have to be enjoying it, too. And then you'll always know what to play next.

"Wow!" Keith said. "Great! I get it. Yeah! I like that!"

"Yeah," Robbie added. "It's kinda like being spontaneous."

"Yes and here's the trick," I confirmed. "You have to really listen to your own show. None of this turning down the monitor and relaxing back 'til the record ends. You have to be your own show's number one fan. This is about being one with the music and above all, having fun. And when

The DJ's of Radio Caroline South
Above: (clockwise) Tom, Rosko Rick Dane, Robbie Dale
Right: (clockwise) Tom, Mike Ahern, Dave Lee Travis, Keith Hampshire, Robbie Dale

you go ashore and do gigs, get involved with the local music scene and bring those experiences to Caroline South and your audience."

Rosko seemed the happiest. "I love it. It's true freedom, it is my greatest dream. Thanks, Tom."

So we went on-the-air with a bang. Our deejays' excitement and exuberance connected with the listeners. We received thousands of fan mail letters thanking us for giving them fun, life and enjoyment. A relationship began to grow between the listeners and the deejays. We were also tying into the historical, British love of the ocean and adventure. Our spirits were high and this seemed to transfer to our audience. The letters we received expressed this enthusiasm.

Some of the deejays would do their shows standing up and dance to the music. The feel of the song then affected the deejay. It was this feeling, more than their words, that was being broadcast. As the audience listened to the deejays and the music, it naturally affected them, slowly bringing to an end the English proper, stiff upper lip.

Every two weeks, if the weather permitted, we would have our shore leave. But the open seas are unpredictable and rough weather was common, often breaking our regular ties to the shore. But that was okay. We enjoyed rocking and rolling on the seas almost as much as we did to the music. If, for any reason at all, there were no replacements, we happily continued to man the turntables.

So, when we were finally able to get shore leave, it became a real treat. There were always crowds of fans, autograph hunters and so many enthusiastic words of encouragement. It was a real feast of merriment, particularly in contrast to the ship's isolation.

Once ashore, I enjoyed catching up with friends, who would fill me in on all the local gossip.

Much more interesting, however, was the dramatic social and cultural changes that were exploding across the country. The girls in their mini skirts advertised an unabashed sexuality, and the guys seemed to have discovered a new confidence with their colorful clothes.

It was as if we were broadcasting energy and excitement from our ships directly into the hearts and minds of millions. It was in this spirit that we decided to host a concert and for the occasion we created a "Caroline Anthem" for people to remember the moment. I was chosen to introduce it.

A theater was booked and invitations were sent out over the air. "Come and join us in a Radio Caroline celebration and learn our new song, and you can also jump and dance to the Hollies."

When I arrived at the venue, dressed in a white suit and a red pencil tie, the hall was already packed and throbbing.

I ran out on stage, introduced myself and Radio Caroline, and then a thirty by fifteen foot screen was lowered. It contained the large lettered words of our anthem:

Caroline. Listen in to Caroline.
If you want the best in entertainment just choose
    Radio Caroline.
Listen in to Caroline it makes you feel alive.
Your all day music station with the sound of '65.
Caroline. Listen in to Caroline.
Caroline. Listen in to Caroline.

If you want the best in entertainment just choose
    Radio Caroline.
Listen in to Caroline.
Get with it at the start.

Your all day friendly station that keeps you young
  at heart.
Caroline. Listen in to Caroline it makes you happy.
Listen in to Caroline.

I had a long stick in my hand and as the music played,
I pointed along to the words. Soon thousands of people
were singing. We sang the anthem a few times and then the
whole audience broke into applause and cheers.
  During the cacophony, the board was pulled up and I
ran over to the microphone, "Now from Manchester, here

Tom and the "Caroline Anthem"

are the Hollies." They came running onstage, Don Rathbone jumped in behind the drums and, with a roll, opened with their number one UK hit, "I'm Alive." The audience went wild, and with the audience clapping and moving, they soon went into their new release, "Look Through Any Window."

I was as excited as the audience. I jumped off the stage and joined them, bobbing to the music. At the end I lingered awhile, mingling with the crowd. I spoke about Caroline, about life onboard, about our adventures and also took requests for my next show. Such was shore leave.

In a few days I was back onboard enjoying the isolation, the swish of the waves on the ship's hull, spinning the records and with the microphone close to my face, speaking directly to all the people I had met. I loved these two contrasting worlds.

I decided it was time that I recreated the Wigan Pier Oil Well Company, but this time, for Caroline South. The question was what to call it. On-the-air I asked, "Where is there, around here, an oily place?"

Many answers came in. I chose Wapping Swamp in cockney East London as the most likely place to discover oil. Soon the Wapping Swamp Oil Well Company was launched and again the subscribers outnumbered my expectations.

As always, the new music continued to arrive. There was "Keep on Running" by the Spencer Davis Group, which shot straight into the number two spot on the charts; "My Generation" by the Who; and one of my favorite American groups, the Four Seasons, with "Let's Hang On!" Caroline South was rocking.

CHAPTER 8

Shipwrecked

January 9, 1966 was cold and stormy. Snow was falling along the coast. That morning I had been playing some good lively music, like the Stones' "Get Off of My Cloud" and "It's My Life" by the Animals, but nothing would warm up the day. The wind kept getting stronger and the ship started to roll and heave. With each wave the whole ship creaked and groaned. Soon we had to secure all the portholes and doors. By evening our little ship was really rolling around in the turbulent North Sea. Norman St. John was seasick, so I took over his shift. I opened with the Beatles' "Day Tripper" and closed with "Eve of Destruction" by Barry McGuire. By the end of the show I was so tired, I had dinner and immediately went to bed.

I was glad to settle into my bunk. It never bothered me that the ship was rolling back and forth. I was fast asleep when DLT burst into my cabin shouting, "Tom! Tom! Wake up!"

"What's up, Dave?" I yawned.

"We're in a storm. The captain wants everyone up in the lounge, packed and ready to leave the ship."

"Yeah, sure." I didn't believe him. We were always playing jokes on each other and DLT had a great sense of humor. Besides, this wind was nothing compared to the storm I had been in on Caroline North. Dave was not going to get a laugh at my expense.

DLT shrugged his shoulders and left. I turned over and went back to sleep. Soon Graham Webb walked in, "Tom, wake up... Come on!"

"What now?" I said.

"Tom, this is serious. Get packed!"

I stretched and yawned. "Hell. Okay." Graham rushed out the door.

I was ready to play the joke. I dressed in my shore clothes, packed my bag and tossed my wolf pelt over my shoulders. I shot and killed that wolf when I was stranded on Great Slave Lake. I called it Mohair Sam.

I scampered up the stairs. In the lounge were Tony Blackburn, Graham Webb, Norman St. John, Dave Lee Travis and the radio engineers George Saunders and Patrick Starling.

"Okay you guys, I'll meet you onshore in the pub," I said. "Last one in pays for everyone's drinks." Everyone seemed to laugh from that.

Suddenly the ship heaved and the main engine raced. A couple of the Dutch crew went running by shouting, "Hode verdomme!" Now I became concerned. This was a serious

Dutch swearword. I went to the bridge to see what was going on. There was Captain Vrury and the chief engineer. "What's happening?" I asked.

The captain turned to me. "The storm has broken our anchor chain and the propellers are full of barnacles. They are unable to create enough thrust to move the ship. The wind is blowing us toward the shore."

I looked out at the dark night and I could see that something was wrong—none of the shore lights looked familiar. We were moving. I went down to the studio. If we were broadcasting inside the three-mile international limit, then we would be breaking the law. I felt that it was important that our audience knew what was happening. I had someone announce that because there was the chance that we

could drift inside the three-mile limit, we were going off-the-air now, but we would resume the broadcast as soon as all was well and we were back out to sea.

After that there was nothing I could do. I would just be in the way. I returned to the lounge and asked DLT if he wanted to play checkers.

Tom and Mohair Sam

He agreed. The last time we played, DLT had beaten me and I did not want that to happen again. We started another intense game. He was good. The game was moving neck and neck, we were each holding ground and it was touch and go as to who would win when the board went flying across the lounge. We heard a loud noise as the ship hit the beach. I had no idea that we were that close to the shore. Everyone scrambled out on deck.

We were broadside to the beach, sitting miraculously between two concrete groins, two buttresses at ninety degrees to the shore. A few feet either way, our ship would have been smashed to pieces. Large waves were crashing over our ocean side, creating the danger that the power of the waves could force our ship over onto its side and possibly dump us all into the freezing cold ocean.

Out on the deck I could see the land covered in snow and a lot of moving lights. There were people running about and inaudible voices shouting. Then I heard a voice

Radio Caroline South on the beach, January 9th 1966

through a megaphone. It was loud and clear, "Stand back! Stand back! We're going to fire a rope! Get off the deck!"

We all ducked back into the cabin and there was a loud bang as a rope came shooting onto the ship. This was grabbed by one of the crew and they set up a pulley system for a breaches buoy, a system for hauling people off ships.

Our crew was instructing us how to get into the breaches buoy. They were like a pair of shorts with a buoy around your waist. You held on the best you could and, in jerks, you were pulled across the waves to the land.

I had grabbed my bag and a large picture of Jeanine, my wife. I climbed into the breaches and as I was hauled across the waves, I bobbed up and down. With each down, I was dunked into the freezing ocean water and arrived cold and wet. The solid, unmoving land felt strange. I was so used to the floor always moving that the firmness of the beach felt unsafe.

There were many hands helping me out of the breaches buoy and a police constable handed me a large cup of hot tea. "This should warm you up," he said with a chuckle. Ah! This was England! Once all of us were off the ship, except the captain and some crew, we were stuffed into a vehicle and driven to a store. We were given dry clothes, courtesy of an association that helped shipwrecked sailors. From there we were taken to a hotel for supper and a welcomed night's sleep.

Early the next morning I received a phone call from Ronan: "Come up to London right away. They want to interview you on *ITN News*."

Everything was moving so quickly. There was a picture

of me being hauled off the ship carrying a four foot picture of Jeanine on the front page of one of the newspapers and I was on the TV. The interviewer asked me to describe the experience.

"We were told to abandon ship," I said as the camera rolled. "When ashore, we were fed and given tea. The poor ship may be battered to pieces by now."

"Is this the end of Caroline South?" he asked.

"Hell no!"

We were the number one news story, but we had no ship. Soon Ronan got a call from Britt Wadner, a Swedish lady who had a radio ship that was not being used. She offered to let us use her ship, the *Cheeta II*, while ours was being repaired. We were back on-the-air.

It was peculiar being on *Cheeta II*. The studio did not have the full, familiar sound of the *Mi Amigo*. We were all impatient for the return of our old friend. When I left for my shore leave, Rosko was on-the-air with his myna bird, the two of them chattering and bantering. As I sailed to shore in the tender, I was listening on a small radio by the boat's wheel. The skipper and I were laughing at his fast-flowing antics. This spontaneity was one of the gems of our programming and especially with an unpredictable myna bird. Rosko was funny. Later on, we took the joke even further. When Rosko was on shore leave, we played a loop tape to the bird so that when Rosko came back and went on-the-air, the bird kept calling Rosko names. Rosko loved it. There was a spirit about the Radio Caroline sound that was contagious. It felt good. It made you feel that life was a joy. Even though we were out on the high seas, living in confined

Caroline's shipwrecked crew

spaces, enjoyment just flowed through our programs. There were so many new experiences always happening that as I docked in Harwich, I was wondering what was waiting for me around the next corner.

RONAN'S STORY

After returning from my shore leave and while the repairs to the *Mi Amigo* were being accomplished, I spent more time at Caroline House with Ronan. One day we were chatting about this and that, and I asked Ronan why he started Radio Caroline.

"That's a good story," he said. "It was all because of Georgie Fame."

"Georgie Fame? Yeah, I had heard that," I said, "but I always wondered what the connection was."

"It all began when I opened a rhythm and blues club named the Scene. One of the groups I had perform at my club were an unknown struggling group from Richmond called the Rolling Stones. I bought the Stones their first set of stage equipment and managed them until Andrew Loog Oldham took over. I also managed Alexis Korner."

I later learned that Ronan was also very influential in the early days of Eric Burdon and the Animals. Legend has it that he suggested the name the Animals.

"At that time I found this young organ player, a great blues musician. 'Okay, Georgie,' I said to him. 'We'll try and get you a record contract.' We recorded a demo of the song 'Yeh Yeh' but all the record companies said his music was too 'black.' So I made the record myself, but the BBC also said it was too 'black' and wouldn't play it. They wouldn't even touch it."

"Everybody sure missed," I said. "I mean, January of last year [1965] it was number one."

"Listen, Tommy baby, it's always like that. The ones who are in control never know what's best."

"So, then what?" I asked.

"All that was left was Radio Luxembourg."

"Old, crackly Radio Luxembourg? But they only play the first minute of each record."

"It was all that was left."

"I had a package with a copy of 'Yeh Yeh' under my arm. I must have looked like a courier or maybe it was my Irish accent, who knows? I walked into the front office and said to the receptionist, 'Which way to Sir Geoffrey Everett's office?' Just like that. I was moving quickly. She pointed to the

Ronan with Patrick Starling

door and before she could say another word, I went straight in. Quick and friendly."

"She didn't try to stop you?" I asked.

"Oh, she might have, but I was too quick. You have to remember that this was my last chance, all the other doors had closed."

"I love it!" I said.

"Now, there I was in the top man's office. There were three desks, a large one with Sir Geoffrey sitting and a small desk on each side with two smaller men sitting. It was all so funny looking. There was a couch in front of the desks. I plunked myself down there. They all looked most surprised. 'Yes?' One of them said. 'What can we do for you?'"

"I held out my package and said, 'I have a record for you to play on your radio station.'"

"All three burst out laughing. Sir Geoffrey got up, went to a curtain on the wall, pulled a cord and revealed a board titled 'Radio Luxembourg's Programming.' Starting at 6:00 p.m., it showed the record company's bookings all the way to closing at 1:00 a.m. 'See,' he said. 'We have no room.'"

"'Well then,' I said, 'I'll have to start my own radio station, won't I?'"

"'How will you do that?' one of them asked."

"'You have a station in Luxembourg, I could put one in France.' You should have seen their faces. And with that, I got up and left. That was the seed, Tommy. That started me thinking and searching how to start a radio station."

"Why Radio Caroline?" I asked. "I mean, it's a great name. How did you get the idea?"

"That's another funny story. I was flying to Dallas, Texas to buy the transmitter and I was reading a magazine, *Time*, *Life*, or something. There was this picture of President Kennedy chasing his daughter around the Oval Office and the caption read, 'Caroline holds up government.' I said to myself, 'That's it! Caroline! Yes, that's it!'"

Ronan paused for a moment, as if searching for the memory. There was a twinkle in his eyes. He started to laugh, "There's another part. When I got back to London, we had a board meeting. It was a little bit stuffy. They had been coming up with all kinds of different names for the radio station. Like Radio Mars or Radio X-ray, they wanted some futuristic sounding name. X was popular at that time. It had to have an X in the name. So when I announced that we were calling it

Radio Caroline, all their jaws dropped. They were appalled. But they were too polite to say anything."

Ronan paused. "Then one of the men came over to me and said in a very fatherly and private way, 'Ronan, if you call it Caroline, they'll think you're queer.'"

We both laughed and I said, "Well, they sure had you wrong and it turned out to be a perfect name."

I walked out of Caroline House and out along Chesterfield Gardens through the passenger underpass to Hyde Park. Someone was playing a flute that echoed through the tunnel, he was playing "Amazing Grace." His playing moved me and I dropped a one pound note in his hat. When I exited the tunnel, the air was cool but the sun was shining on my face. There were two girls and a guy sitting under a tree listening to a transistor radio. I could hear the Hollies' "I Can't Let Go." When the song ended, there was the familiar voice of DLT. Radio Caroline was alive and everywhere.

"Great radio," I said to them.

"Yes, it's the best," one of them said with a smile.

In two years, London had changed from a dark, dank land owned by the privileged into a creative city of opportunity. Music was pouring out from everywhere. We were being swamped with records from bands we had never heard of. A current had become a fast-moving torrent and we were riding on top of it. Even though Radio Caroline had been shipwrecked and was in repair, it felt like nothing could ever stop us.

CHAPTER 9

Paul McCartney Plans a Family Outing

In March 1966 we were still broadcasting from the *Cheeta II*, but going strong. The Hollies, the Yardbirds, the Animals and the Stones were all on the UK charts. The Troggs came out with "Wild Thing." A group called the Mindbenders had a big hit with "A Groovy Kind of Love". The Americans were popular; the Four Seasons had a hit with "Let's Hang On!" and the Beach Boys had another success with "Barbara Ann."

On the 25th, I received a message to call Ronan on the ship's radio. He seemed very animated.

"What's going on Ronan?"

"Come ashore as fast as possible!"

"Is something wrong?"

"No, it's an important assignment."

"An assignment?"

"A special, secret meeting," Ronan said. "I can't explain it now. Come right away. The tender is on its way to get you. Someone will pick you up onshore. They'll have a microphone and a tape recorder for you. Don't ask any more questions. Just come."

Before I could ask anything else, Ronan had signed off.

When we docked in Harwich there was a black limousine waiting. The chauffeur deposited me in the backseat then got behind the wheel.

"Where are we going?"

"I'm told it's top secret." He smiled as we raced off down the highway.

I could see we were heading in the direction of London, so I decided to relax and enjoy the comfort and soft leather of the vehicle.

My driver started to chat. "You guys are really doing a fantastic job out there."

"Yeah! We're having a ball! You know I can't believe how this country is so total in their support for us," I said.

"Well, you know, Tom, millions and millions of people can't be wrong. My admiration goes out to you guys. This is one of the best things that has ever happened to this bloody country."

"Yes, thanks. We are really lucky, you know. The British people are very special. Without their support, we would've been off-the-air a year ago."

In London we headed for Chelsea. I watched the street names, still wondering where we were going. We drove down the King's Road and turned into a mews. I just caught the name. The Vale.

"This is it," driver said. He pointed, "Through that door."

There was a plain black door. Everything else was brick. Well this certainly was mysterious. I trusted Ronan but I normally liked to prepare before any interviews, get to the core of my subject. On the way over I could have thought up an interesting question or two.

I opened the black door, went through a small plain paved yard and entered a large white studio.

"Oh good, Tom, there you are. I'm Tony Barrow." We shook hands.

"Pleasure to meet you Tony. What's this all about?"

"I work for Brian Epstein. I'm his publicist. We cooked up an idea for an insert in Brian's Music Echo magazine. It's going to feature a lot of stars."

"Sounds great," I said, holding up my recorder. "Who am I interviewing?"

Tony nodded. "We're going to get started shortly. Set up your interview equipment here."

He led me into a white, empty room. It had hardwood floors and posts, and no furniture except for one stool. There looked to be another entrance, but that door was closed.

I was about to point out to Tony that he hadn't answered my question when a young woman entered. She was probably in her early twenties, had long black hair, blue eyes and one of those smiles that makes you stop whatever you are doing. She wore a tight-fitting mini dress and red tights. For a moment I thought I should just forget the interview.

Tony introduced me to her, Nancy. She was a CBC reporter. I stuttered about Radio Caroline and the CBC. I'm not sure she was even listening.

The door opened behind me with laughter and voices. I turned and saw a group enter. For a split second I assumed they were just more visitors passing through, but at once it hit me. They were the Beatles.

I should have figured it out. Brian Epstein, the secrecy. But I didn't have any time for that now—or Nancy, who had vanished in any case.

"Hi, guys! What a knockout! Fancy meeting you here! I thought I was going to interview the Queen, but I guess you'll do." They laughed and we all shook hands.

Paul McCartney, George Harrison and Ringo Starr were wearing black suits. Paul and Ringo had on black turtleneck shirts, George was in a white open collared shirt. John Lennon was dressed a little differently with a navy sports jacket, white trousers and a white shirt. They looked very smart. Their hair was neat in their mop-tops.

I sat on a stool with them standing around me. I turned on the small reel-to-reel tape recorder. At this point my plan was simple—just record and see what came out. Whatever happened was fine.

"Right, well, this is the big recording session with the four, the big four that is, the one and only Paul, John, George and Ringo. How about that?"

John leaned into microphone saying, "The Baffle Brothers. For recording. The baffles."

"Thank you very much indeed, John," I said. "Now I'd like a few words from you my friend."

John smiled. "Well eh, it's nice to be here in the actual

captain's kitchen. And the captain himself is stirring up a right old brew."

This was going to be interesting. "Thank you very much indeed," I said. "You know what this is for? This is for the little paper called *Disc and Music Echo*."

Brian Epstein's role in the Beatles success is legendary. However at one time or another he managed additional acts, like Gerry & the Pacemakers, Cilla Black and others. His music paper was, in part, a vehicle for supporting these groups.

John was not impressed. He nodded. "Music Disc. Em. Yes."

"And it's going to be one of the biggest productions across the country," I added.

"Biggest," John said sarcastically, putting his hands on his hips. "Big. Lot of push behind it. A lot of big people behind that, yeah. A lot of big people behind that."

I wondered for a moment what the lads knew about the purpose of the interview. I decided to join in the fun of the moment. I put on the weird voice of Peter Sellers' Bluebottle character from the old BBC comedy, *The Goon Show*.

"Yeaas matey, yeaas," I said, then switched back to my ordinary voice. "And how about you Paul? Tell me a bit about music writing."

"Yes, um… well… I'm still… writing…" Paul hesitated. He smiled and stepped back.

"Thank you very much," I said. I knew I had to keep the conversation moving since I did not have a hint of how much time I would be given. I hadn't even thought about how much tape was available on the recorder.

I turned to Ringo. "Okay, Mr. Ringo."

"Yes?" he answered, opening his hands.

"What's it like being a Beatle?"

"It's okay, you know," Ringo shrugged.

"It's okay?"

"Yeah. It's okay."

I needed a little more than this. I tried again. "Tell me a bit about what's it like being a married man and a Beatle?"

Ringo put both hands up in false glee, laughing, "It's okay, it's okay. Uh. Ha ha ha."

Nothing more. I was getting nothing. In frustration I blurted out, "You're leaving me right in the middle of it, eh?" I pointed the microphone toward George. "Well, I know George will say..."

"Hello, hello, hello."

John laughed and said, "Hello there, George."

I was feeling a little awkward just sitting, holding a microphone. What to do now? I said to the group, "What do you think of this microphone I'm using?"

George leaned in. "It's very nice George, very nice microphone," he said as if he were talking to himself. He looked at me. "But the listeners can't really see it, can they?"

In searching for material to use I fell back on the obvious, "You're planning, right now, a new LP—I understand." This had been in all the music papers.

"We're not," George said without hesitation. "We haven't planned any, you know, we just sort of..." he hesitated and then tried to explain.

"They tried to write a few songs," he said pointing to John and Paul. "And then we would gather together and emerge with an LP. But we never sort of plan it and say, 'This is what it's gonna be fellows.'"

"Do you plan, eh...?"

John interrupted, put his hand on my arm, smiling. "We're engaged but we're not planning anything. We're not planning, we're not planning. We're engaged, yes, but not planning."

I turned to Paul, "I understand that you're engaged, Paul."

"Well, we're just good friends, all of us. Good friends," he said.

"I'm so glad to hear that."

As if remembering something, Paul looked at me, smiling but stern, "Let's leave it at that and no more comment."

"Tell me something Paul, do you have a policy for your work or do you just play it off the top of your head?"

Paul put both hands behind his head and then up in the air and said, "Just off the top of our heads, Tom. You know, just for kicks."

"You're sure of that?" I asked.

"Sure. Plain deal."

John jumped in, twirling his hands around and blurted out, "Hallucinations."

"Sure, sure," agreed Paul, "you know purple hearts."

John added, "You know all them pop groups take 'em."

Paul agreed, "Yeah."

"Do you John?" I asked.

"Naw, never touch them," answered John.

I pointed to Ringo. "I don't think Ringo knows what they are."

"No, I don't," he agreed.

"I like bonanzas," said John.

"What are bonanzas?" I asked.

He shrugged, "I just made it up in case there's any vicars listening."

I did not know much about drugs, but it didn't stop me from asking. "What about morning glory seeds?"

John looked disgusted. "I haven't seen any. I wouldn't fancy eating a flower, even for the laugh." And with that they all busted out laughing.

"Okay," I said.

Paul clapped his hands together. "Okay, how about that, a big hand."

John twisted and turned as he talked nonsense, "Have a bib... B... Wee! Hello."

I honked my Model T Ford car horn, which I had brought along.

Paul grabbed the microphone. He spoke with a false American radio voice, "This is Ed Morrow of the big L. Hello, Ed. How are you, okay? And the swing along with the disc jockey show."

It was all turning into a chaotic soup. I wanted to bring the interview back down to earth. "I know something that the people would like to know is, what's your mail that you get in quantity?"

But John was not going to allow any seriousness. "Well we had a nice little male the other day, he was about five-foot-three and he came around with the bread."

What to do now? I just said, "Thank you very much," and added, "that was, of course, John."

John looked serious. "No, it wasn't!" He turned to the others, "He's lying to you. Propaganda you see. Learn the truth between difference."

"Well, you see, John, I was just trying to be a good PR man."

Paul said, "Right. Thank you."

John slapped me on the back, looking sympathetic and friendly. "You are a good PR man."

"What kind of mail response do you get Mr. Ringo?"

"Eh... It's okay. It's okay."

I was almost pleased with his unresponsiveness. Maybe it would lead to a little sanity. "Do you answer every one?"

"No, not every one. We're too busy for that. We'd like to, you know, but we just need more time."

But Ringo's sudden seriousness was too much and they all burst out laughing.

"Oh well for the boy who's laughing," John said.

In silence they all stopped, waiting almost in a whisper. George said, "I've nothing in particular of anything at all."

John began speaking in a serious voice. "Well, here as we are gathered here today..."

"Paul," I interrupted, "you are the only single Beatle at this stage. Now, how long is this going to last, man?"

"Well," said Paul, laughing and then turning serious as he poked me in the chest, "it could last for any amount of time, really. As soon as the divorce comes through and the kids are set straight, then I'll be able to move on and continue with my plans. And God bless all of us."

"What are your plans?" I asked him.

Paul turned his head to one side, as if deep in thought.

"Well, I don't know really. I haven't got any plans and that's what I'm saying and I've got no plans."

"Thank you," I said. "And what are your plans for the future as regards to space travel?" I don't know where I came up with that.

Not surprisingly, Paul looked puzzled. "Well um, I hadn't thought about it too deeply up to now."

George answered for him, "The need to split our own atoms, you know, and sort of get into Chicago in ten minutes."

"I'm all for that." Paul nodded his head.

Then George went on. "You know, not this traveling."

I understood his distaste. I was sure that the Beatles must be continuously on the road and in airports.

"And how are you going to do that, George?" I asked.

"Oh, it's all, you know, it's all in...it's all in the book, you got to learn it, sort of..."

I wasn't sure I had nearly enough for the magazine production, so I tried a new tactic. "Tell me, is the rumor true that you are going to set up a satellite pirate radio station?" I asked George.

"Um, no, untrue."

"Filthy lies," John said.

"Propaganda again," George added.

"I wonder who started that one."

"I think it was him, from Butlins," said John. Butlins is an English summer holiday camp. But who on earth was this "him?" I had no idea.

"I think that one was started by Ringo, wasn't it?" I said.

"No, that wasn't by me," I was sure he was being genuinely defensive.

"No?" I said with disbelief.

"No, it was by you," retorted Ringo.

"Ah yes, it could be," I accepted.

"Blue Bayou." Paul said out of nowhere. I assumed he was referring to Roy Orbison's hit "Blue Bayou," but why, I had no idea. I couldn't think of anything to say to that, so I started blowing my horn. And John began to sing "dah, dah dah." Then they all put their heads together and started to sing, in harmony, a lively wordless song.

But they were not in tune with my horn. "You got to get the right key for that one," I said.

"Gonna blast it," Paul said as he grabbed my horn and gave it a honk.

"That was Paul, of course," I calmly said.

John pointed at Paul, "He should give us something in his high voice."

I thought it was a great idea. "Paul give us something in your high voice."

"Naw," said Paul, "I couldn't think of any appropriate tune, really."

George turned to me and said, "Play a request for us, uh?"

They all jumped in, crowding close to me, pretending to be groupies. "Yeah!"

"Play a request," repeated George.

"We'll play a request for you," I said. "We'll play lots of requests if you like."

"Okay. 'The Green Door,'" Paul said, jumping up and down with excitement and clapping his hands.

"Green door?"

"The B-side," John said. "'Priscilla.'"

Paul started to sing. "Priscilla, put that ring on your finger, Priscilla. That one."

"Come on, let's have some more," I pleaded. "I don't recognize that one."

Paul raised his hand. "Oh, it's great, it's terrible,"

"The worst thing to come out of England," John said in a very dull voice. That seemed to bring down the energy.

It occurred to me that the way the Beatles acted together here—their manner of speaking, the way they behaved or maybe misbehaved, and the way they interacted with each other—was the same as they were in their music. Ringo was solid and steady, the drummer. John and Paul played off each other, just as they did in their singing and songwriting. George was there in the background coming in every now and again with lead guitar licks. It was as if there was no difference between their music and their lives together. No wonder they were so good. No wonder they were so successful. It all flowed together in the same way, whether they were on or off the stage.

Any more insight would have to wait. I still had to bring them back to this project I was given. Then I remembered that Radio Caroline's birthday was coming up in three days.

"First of all, it is Radio Caroline's birthday on the 28th," I said. "I wonder if you would all make a 'Happy Birthday' to our good ship out there at sea."

Without hesitation, they all cooperated.

"Happy birthday, Caroline," Paul said.

John hammed it up. "Happy birthday goody, good ship out at sea."

George was next, "Happy birthday everyone on the good ship Caroline."

Then finally Ringo. "Happy birthday, Caroline. It's been wonderful."

"Do you ever listen to Caroline, John?" I asked.

He put his hand to his chin. "Uh, never find it actually."

"Where is it?" asked Ringo.

"It's 199," I said.

"Oh, yes," John said as if remembering, "I've listened to it, yes."

"That's that one," added Paul.

"That's right," I confirmed. "Now tell me, are you all Alfies?" *Alfie* was a hit movie with Michael Caine about a young, working-class man who lives only for physical relationships with beautiful women. So I was asking if this was their lifestyle.

"No, no, no," they all said with certainty.

"You're not all Alfies?" I said pressing the point. "Surely you are all promiscuous with all these groupies throwing themselves at you."

Ringo was not going to allow me to continue down that road. "No," he said, "Protestant."

"Ringo's a Protestant," I said as a statement, not a question.

"I'm proud of it!"

"Yes," was all I could say.

But now it was time for another subject and back to Caroline. "Anyway, how would you like to be a disc jockey at sea?"

"Um," Paul said. "I wouldn't like to be... Well maybe... I wanted to be."

"You wanted to be?"

"No... I thought of it."

John looked at Paul. "You could play a few records in between your bass." Then he mimicked someone becoming nauseated. "And throwing up all over your records as you were trying to play them." John turned to me and put his hand over his mouth as if he were telling me a secret, "I think they're all queer, you know, those fellows on the boats."

It was all very amusing but wasn't doing me much good. I was really beginning to worry that I was running out of time.

I turned to Ringo. "When did you first have sex, Ringo?"

Without any concern he answered, "Oh... I don't remember."

John was eager to answer, "When I was about three, I think."

George wagged his finger. "They called it 'diddy-winky.'"

"Paul, when did you first have sex?" I asked.

"When I was about five, in the woods."

"And you George?"

"When I was about thirty-three, in the woods," he said.

"These are very lucky woods, aren't they?" I piped in.

"They were at school together," John said with a smirk.

"They were?"

I got an idea. I recalled meeting Lance Percival, the co-median and actor, on Carnaby Street. He had done voices of

Paul and John in a cartoon called *The Beatles*. I asked John if he would turn the tables and do an imitation of Lance.

John knew right away that it wasn't such a good idea. He shook his head. "I couldn't do Lance, he does it so well himself, I couldn't do Lance, oh no."

Now I felt it was time to squash some of those rumors that were floating around the gossip papers. "Is it true, Paul and John, that you have ghostwriters to write your songs for you? "

"Oh, yeah," Paul said, nodding his head. "Ghostwriters."

"We got ghost Will an' Trotsky. They write the first four." John quickly joined in.

"And Lenin and Blavatsky, they write the lyrics," Paul continued. "The two best-selling lyric writers in the country," he added with conviction.

John, looking serious, continued. "We just do the PR for the boys, you know."

"Yeah," Paul said, puffing out his chest, "we just do the appearances in our mop-tops, you know."

"Yeah. It's a hard life, isn't it?" I agreed.

"Yeah," said John. "It's very hard, but we just wander around. We got doubles for most of that as well."

"You have, eh?" I said.

"We got people that look like Elvis Presley in our camp as well," John insisted. "So he's no trouble to us, you see."

"That's cool."

"And people that look like gorillas," added Paul. "So that when people see them, they think, 'Ah ha, there are those dressed up as gorillas.'"

"Right."

John frowned. "All this is going on to confuse the mind, you see, while we're getting away from the associated object."

Paul announced, "I'm working all my equipment for the ultimate good of humankind."

Half of me was having fun with all this teasing and the other half was concerned that I would not have enough material. All four of them resisted my interjecting any seriousness into the interview. Whatever tactic I tried, it wound up as a joke.

I decided to just have fun with whatever time I had remaining.

"Do you think, George, that Ugly Ray Teret is really ugly?"

"Who?" asked George. "Ugly Red Terror?"

"Ugly Ray Teret," I replied.

"I don't know Ugly Ray Teret."

"No, Ray's okay," said Ringo.

I was surprised. "You know Ray?"

"I know Ray. Good old Ray. Ray Teret," said Ringo.

"He shaved his hair off," I informed.

"Who is he?" asked George.

"He's a disc jockey," I said.

"Oh, yeah."

"Caroline North," I added.

George's face suddenly lit up and with vigor he said, "Ugly Ray Teret! Great!"

John swooped in with enthusiasm. "Ugly Ray Taylor. Keep playing them Ugly."

I realized that I may be able to get them to do some promos that our deejays could use on their shows. "I wonder if you would say a few words to some of the fellows. First of all, Mike Ahern."

Looking unsure, George asked, "Michael Hern?"

"Mike Ahern."

George confirmed, "Ahern."

"He's from Liverpool," I said.

"Mike Ahern. Hello, Mike. How are you? Okay?" George said.

Ringo spoke up, "Hello, Mike Ahern, keep playing them."

Paul put on a serious face, very scholarly-like. "Hello, Mike, well here we are. It's not such a different occasion as it ever was, but here we are to wish you a few words on behalf of the boys and myself. Thank you."

"Thank you, Michael," John said.

"Thank you, John," I said. "And one for Murph the Surf."

Paul laughed, "Oh, Murph the Surf."

"Oh yeah," John said sarcastically, "and one for Ted the Red."

Paul wasn't finished, "Good old Murph the Surf. Good old Murph the Surf."

Ringo said, "Hello, Murph the Surf. Keep surfing Murph."

"Hello, Murph the Surf," said George.

"Okay, we also have a fellow on Caroline South from Manchester called DLT or Dave Lee Travis."

"Dave Lee Travis," said Paul.

"Bring it on," said Ringo.

"A big hand for Dave Lee Travis," said George.

Finally, with gusto, John said, "Hey, Dave Lee Travis, hey, take it away."

"Right," I said, "and don't forget Tony Blackburn on Caroline South."

They all jumped in with, "And a big hand...bring him on...five pounds..."

"Say hello to him," I insisted.

Ringo leaned into to the microphone, "Hello, Tony Blackburn."

"Right," I said. Now it was my turn. "And how about giving me a hello."

"Giving you a hello? Hello!" said George.

"Hello. Bring him on, a big hand," added Paul.

"Hello," said John.

"Good old Tommy," cheered Ringo.

"Thank you," I said.

Paul added, "Hello. Yes, hello Tommy."

"Tommy forever," said Ringo.

I really didn't mind being called Tommy, but on Caroline I was strictly Tom. "Actually they only call me Tom."

That was fine with John. "Tom from Texas. Texas Tom," he said.

Then Paul joined in, "Great to have worked with you, Tom, great to have worked with you, Tom."

"Yes," I said, "and we'll keep spinning your discs."

John said, "And we'll keep spinning your discs, Tom."

"That's the only way we can keep on-the-air, you see."

"Well that's nice to know," agreed John.

"Otherwise we'd lose our audience."

Paul suddenly got serious, very much all business. He put his hand on my shoulder. "Paying your PRS? All you boats...and we'll support you."

PRS was the Performing Right Society, the organization that radio stations paid for the right to play the music. The money collected was shared with the composers, writers and publishers. This was a substantial amount of revenue through which John and Paul received over and above their record sales.

I reassured them. "We pay PRS."

"Do you?" John seemed to doubt me.

"Great," Paul said. "Big hand. Bring him on."

"We've been paying it for the last year," I added.

All four said, "Yeah?"

Paul asked, "How you fixed for electricity?"

John asked, "Are you on a protection racket?"

George added, "How you off for protection?"

"Protection?" I did not understand.

Paul took what was really a joke further. Looking and talking like a Mafia gangster, he said, "Send the boys out, wreck the ship. Twenty-five quid we want. Twenty-five quid a week. Send the boys out. Kill the bleeding lot of you."

I knew how to end this sort of banter. "That was Paul, by the way," I said.

"Oh no," he couldn't get out fast enough.

Now it was time for a new subject. "When are you making another film."

"Ah, we don't know yet," said Paul. "No, we haven't got a script yet."

"We haven't got a script yet," repeated George.

"We haven't got a script yet," added Ringo, nodding his head.

"We haven't got a script yet, either," said John.

Well that seemed clear. "I reckoned they haven't got a script yet," I said.

"No script," said Paul.

"No," agreed John.

Again George said, "We haven't got a script yet."

Paul looked straight at me. "We'd like Caroline North to send a request out. Special request to Donny Andrews."

All of them enthusiastically, "Oh, yeah! To Donny Andrews."

Paul said, "Remove for himself, Andrews."

John said, "Donny, slap that bass."

George added, "And tow that barge."

I had no idea who Donny Andrews was, so I tried to change the subject. Also, I didn't want to ignore my current ship. "I wonder if you'd like to send a request out on Caroline South?"

Again all said, "Yes! To Donny 'slap that bass' Andrews."

"And Mrs. Donny 'slap that bass' Andrews," said George. "And little 'slap that bass.'"

In the sixties, many rock stars kept it secret if they were married so that young women would imagine they had a chance to be with them. But the Beatles broke this policy. It was known that Ringo already had a child.

I asked him, "What's it like being a father?"

"It's great."

I hoped for more. "It's great?" I repeated.

"Oh, it really is great."

"Do you change nappies?"

"Oh no, no." He paused, looked at me accusingly and asked, "Did you?"

"...Never mind."

I turned to George, "When are you going to be a father, George?"

"I don't know," he said. "When are you?"

Paul turned to George and pointed at me, "He is. Three times. Three cheers. Two twins."

I asked, "Who got twins?"

"My little twins," joked Paul.

"You got twins?" I said laughing.

"Down in Bromsbrey," said Paul, increasing his Liverpool accent. "Have you seen them? Little twins down in Bromsbrey. Lovely little couple. Boy and girl. Identical, split as peas, couldn't see the difference. Wonderful little two."

"How old are they?" I asked.

"Four and five."

Everyone laughed. I turned to John, "When are you going to write another book, John?

He already had two published books—of poems, short stories and illustrations—to his credit.

"Well," said John, deepening his voice, "a lot of people have come up to me and said, 'When you going to write another book, John?'" He then paused and said, "I don't know."

"That's a pretty good answer."

John nodded to me and said, "Thank you."

I wanted to come back to the music. "Have you got a plan for a new release?" I asked.

"Um?" said John.

"Have we?" said Paul. "Yes, we have. We're going to record soon, next week or two."

Good. I looked to John for confirmation. "We're getting a single out. We're getting a single out, yeah. We're getting Billy J. Kramer to write one for us."

I knew that it was the other way round, that John and Paul wrote songs for Billy J. Kramer. So to stay with their joke I said, "I thought these two ghostwriters of yours would write it for you."

"No, no," said Paul.

"Not this one?" I asked, playing along.

"No, they're not writing this one," said Paul.

Nothing made sense. "This is going to be your first one?" I asked.

"Yes."

"That's cool," I replied.

Suddenly George interrupted, "Who do you fancy for the National?"

The National was an annual British steeplechase race. The whole nation would listen, stopping everything that they were doing.

"Rough Tweed," said John

"Rough Tweed? Ten to one?" added George.

"More than that," insisted John.

George continued, "More than that? Big Field?"

"Big Strong, Big Field," agreed John.

"Take Strong on the race before," advised George.

I didn't know too much about the race, but went along with their banter. "How much money do you plan to put on the National?"

"Ten Bob each way," said George.

"Ten Bob each way?" I queried.

"Yeah," said George.

Time for a new question. "If you were at sea..."

Ringo interrupted me, touching the microphone and looking me straight in the eyes with concern. "Why don't you get a better mic than that, Tom?"

"I agree. This is the one they sent, you see. I didn't get this one. It looks like the Leaning Tower of Pisa."

Ringo had a solution. "Why don't you do a raffle on the ship you're on and get a good mic?"

"Have you ever been out to Caroline?" I asked him.

"No, I've never been to Caroline," he added with a smile, "I've been to Tobago and Greece and that. Never been to Caroline."

"When are you going to come out to Caroline?" I asked George.

"I'm not," he said with a shudder. "I'm never going to Caroline because I don't like boats. I don't mind them being on the boat, but I don't like personally being on boats.

"Do you get seasick then?" I asked.

"No."

"What about you Paul?" I asked. "You going to come out?"

Falling back into his strong Liverpool accent he said, "Yeah, me and the missus. We'll probably be out there Saturday."

John leaned in, "Take the twins."

Paul nodded, "Probably be out there on Saturday with the twins. Take the little nippers. Do them a world of good, you know, a bit of fresh air out there on the boat."

"That's for sure," I agreed. "How long do you reckon you can stay?"

Paul bent forward, hunched over a little, "Oh, probably a couple of days we'd stay. Come home for the night, you know, lovely."

I said to Paul, "You like Dutch cooking, do you?"

"Oh yeah, love it."

"Plenty of that," I said, smiling at my own inside joke.

"You know they always say cuisine in Dutch, wonderful," said Paul.

"When are you going to come out, John, out to Caroline?"

John wrinkled his brow and looked up as if he were trying to figure it out, "I'll be trying to fit it in somewhere in 1990."

"1990?"

"I think I got Caroline down for 1990," said John.

"You don't like boats?" I asked.

"I like them fine," he said. "Yes, but they are so far away from where I live."

I thought maybe a little competition might get them out to the ship. "We nearly got the Stones out there," I said.

"Did you?" asked Paul, surprised.

"Yeah."

"Good luck to you," replied Paul, shacking me off.

"Couldn't make it though," I said.

"Oh, no," Paul simply said.

John turned to me and tapped me on the chest. "They're not going out there, are they?"

I confessed. "No."

Then suddenly he pushed the others aside, glared at me and shouted in a high voice. He was joking, but a little menacing. "So why do you want us to go out? What are you trying to do?"

Abruptly, everything stopped. There was complete silence. I was aware of a few people now in the room. They were staring. "Well," I explained, "I think that makes all the difference doesn't it?" I felt awkward and embarrassed.

John's face changed from glaring to warm sincerity. He started speaking like somebody's grandfather. He put his arm around me. "Well Tom...you know as well as I do... that Britain depends on people like...Caroline, for annual resources and the prices and income of which I knew will bring you."

Everyone relaxed. "Who's going to win the election?" I asked.

Ringo offered a cigarette. No one replied.

"Who's going to win the election, Ringo?"

"I've no idea, no idea."

George said, "Tony Barrow."

I looked around, but Tony was not in the room.

"Who's going to win the election," I again repeated.

Paul said, "Drakes Drum. Drakes Drum." This meant nothing to me.

John said, "I think Harold Macmillan will get in by a half nelson."

Harold Macmillan had been the British Prime Minister

from 1957 to 1963. But had since retired from politics. He was not even in the running.

Everyone laughed.

I asked John, "You have no political views?"

"No, no, I've got a golf course."

I had no idea what he was talking about.

Paul seemed to know. "It's all those houses, cut it out."

"That's what you reckon?" I said.

John answered, "That's what I reckon, and the first one that gets in, good luck to 'em."

I had lost control. John had a way of derailing whatever I asked. But I was not going to give up. I said to John, "Do you have any ideas as how you'd like to change this country in any way?"

"Yes," said John, "I'd like to change it a lot."

"In what way?"

"Well the tax problem," he said.

"What would you do with the tax?"

"I'd reduce it drastically."

"That's if you were the Chancellor of the Exchequer?" I asked.

"No," he said with disdain. "If I was anybody, I'd reduce it...drastically."

George came pushing in close and, like he was joining in a chorus at the top of his voice, said, "Give the pop stars a fairer share of the country's wealth."

I turned to George. "If you were in politics, that's what you would do?"

"Yes," he said. And then with a twinkle he added, "And any boy that can swim like that ought to be in England's team."

I turned to Ringo, "What would you do if you were in politics to help the country?"

"Oh, I don't know."

"Go on," John encouraged. "Tell them."

"I don't know. No."

John was shaking his hands, "They can't take the taxes down because they haven't got enough money. And they'll never have enough money while they're buying all that crap. Like F-one-one-ones, Harold. Which they've proved are no use whatsoever 'cause we not all...you know, what good's all that? So, if they pay off a few of the bloody debts, then maybe they'd be able to cut the tax down a little, Harold?"

Harold Wilson was the current British Prime Minister.

George chimed in, "What you gonna do about Decca?"

"What about Decca?" I asked.

"Nothing," said George.

Paul said, "Double Decker."

Again they had fallen into the zany. I turned to John and asked, "What's your attitude towards commercial radio on land?"

"I don't mind where it comes from as long as it's there."

Paul agreed, "Yes, I think I'd go along with that, I think. You might as well have it in the middle..."

John interrupted, "Get the local angle, you know." He was alluding to the ideal of having many local radio stations.

"Ey, yes," said Paul. "Get the local angle."

"You'd like to see local commercial stations?" I asked.

"I wouldn't like to see them," said John shaking his head, "I'd just like to hear them."

"Thank you very much." I swung the microphone. "Ringo?"

"Yeah, I would... The more stations the merrier, I always say. You've heard me say it before."

George touched me on the shoulder and said, "Well, I think if the BBC can be legal on land, then so can everybody else. You know, that's how it should be, either they have nobody doing it or they have everybody doing it. Not just the fave, rave, little BBC government-sponsored or whatever it is."

John agreed, "All one-sided, you know."

"You believe in free enterprise, of course, then?" I asked.

John said shaking his head, "I believe in...if something is going to be illegal, then it is illegal for everybody, it isn't just for the government. It's not just all them. Bloody politicians."

Their photographer, Bob Whitaker, was waving his camera at me trying to get my attention. It was time to end.

"Can you all say goodbye now?" I said.

John repeated my tone. "Goodbye now."

Ringo said politely, "Goodbye, Tom. Goodbye, Caroline."

"Thank you very much, Ringo," I said.

George came forward and took the microphone. "Goodbye, Tom, goodbye. Very nice seeing you."

"Thank you, George. Over to Paul."

Paul looked warmly at me, "Goodbye, Tom. Goodbye, Holy Red Terror and all the rest of you. Goodbye."

John put out his hand to shake mine, "Goodbye, Tom, Caroline, you know...all them."

"Thank you very much indeed, John."

"Wonderful, wonderful," he said.

"Right," I said. "Well, I think we'll call that a day and we look forward to seeing you very, very soon in the future. Thank you very much indeed, all of you."

I turned off the tape recorder. It had not run out. Still holding the microphone and sitting on the stool, we were posed together, with Paul and George on my right and John and Ringo on my left while Bob Whitaker flashed a few photographs. I gave my horn a few blasts, we all laughed one last time and then Tony Barrow led me out.

I learned later that this had been the infamous "butcher" cover photographic session for the soon to be released American album, the Beatles' *Yesterday and Today*. Bob Whitaker had taken the shots of torn dolls and bloody meat. But this was too much for Capitol Records, USA and the cover was replaced with some bland pictures of the four.

The limousine drove me back to Harwich and the tender took me back out to Caroline.

When I arrived, Mike Ahern and Dave Lee Travis were there on deck to meet me.

"Where did you go?" asked Mike.

"What a trip!" I said.

"Why? What happened?" asked Dave.

"I just can't believe what just happened."

"What?" they both said together.

"I interviewed the Beatles."

"Bullshit," said Mike. "Really?"

"Listen," I said, "let me get settled and I'll tell you all about it."

SOUND OF THE STARS!

IT was all very mysterious and very few
people knew what was going on. Suddenly,
without warning, Radio Caroline's top deejay
TOM LODGE was whipped off the pop ship
last Friday and rushed into London for a hush-
hush get-together with THE BEATLES.

At a Chelsea studio close to King's Road,
Lodge spent an hour with John, Paul, George,
Ringo . . . and a tape recorder!

For the story that goes with our special
picture, make sure you see next week's issue
of MUSIC ECHO and read the first exciting
details about SOUND OF THE STARS!

I dropped my stuff in my cabin and then came back up to the lounge. They had a cup of tea waiting for me. Robbie Dale had joined them. I pulled up a chair.

"What a crazy way of doing things," I said. "You know that Brian Epstein and crew are so secretive and protective with the Beatles. I can't believe it."

"Well, they have to be," said Robbie. "If not, those poor guys will never have any peace."

"Yeah, I know," I answered. "But still, they could have let me know so that I could have had some questions prepared. And besides, those guys are a non-stop lark. They never stop being crazy."

"What do you mean?" asked Dave.

"The only one that would answer a question seriously was Ringo and he was boring. John and Paul are a comedy team and George was..."

"What do you have on the recording?" asked Robbie. "Can you use what you have?"

"I hope so. Tony Barrow, the Beatles' publicist, gave me some recordings of interviews. Cilla Black, Cliff Richard, Spencer Davis, Dusty Springfield, Pete Townshend and others are on it. I'm to make a production with these and the Beatles for Disc and Music Echo. But here is the sticker, I cannot use any music. I guess they don't want to have to pay copyright."

"Wow!" said Mike. "That sounds like fun."

"Yes," I agreed, "and it's to be called *Sound of the Stars*. How have things been while I was away?"

Dave shrugged, "Oh you know, music, food, waves, seagulls and the occasional passing ship. But otherwise nothing, just fun."

We all laughed. I went back down to my cabin and from the speaker came the Beatles' number one hit, "Day Tripper."

The next morning was cool and wet. My morning show was a chance for me to warm up the country. I spoke about my adventures with the Beatles, reminding the listeners to be sure to keep an eye out for the magazine and the disc of my interview.

After breakfast I buckled down in the library, editing the tape to create a production for Tony Barrow, Brian Epstien and *Disc and Music Echo*.

With a tape recorder, editing block, razor blade, splicing tape, wax marking pencil, eight reels of recordings of interviews and an LP containing sound effects, I carefully organized myself at the table.

I had Cilla Black speaking with the Bachelors; Cliff Richard talking to Hank Marvin and Bruce Welch of the Shadows; Penny Valentine from the BBC's *Juke Box Jury* speaking

WANT A RECORD featuring the voices of the Beatles, Walkers, Cilla, Hollies, Cliff, the Who, Sandie, Seekers, Shadows, Tom Lodge, Adam Faith, Cathy McGowan, Dusty, Spencer, and the Bachelors —FREE? See page 9

SOUND of the STARS
A FANTASTIC OFFER
TO DISC WEEKLY READERS

Page from *Disc and Music Echo* with photo of Tom in the back with Cathy McGowan and the Hollies

with Judith Durham of the Australian group, the Seekers; Cathy McGowan from ITV's show *Ready, Steady, Go!* talking with the Hollies; Dusty Springfield chatting with Spencer Davis; Pete Townshend of the Who, the Walker Brothers, as well as John and Gary speaking with Penny Valentine; Adam Faith speaking with his discovery, Sandy Shaw; and, of course, my Beatles interview.

I was not to use any copyrighted music, but I could use sound effects. I was to make a compact production for a small two-sided disc made of thin plastic and bound into the magazine. I only had a few minutes to make it sensational and exciting.

Of course, nobody could top the Beatles with their eleven UK releases, nine number one hits and six albums. So I decided to begin with an enticement, a taste of the Beatles, a little hysteria, and then follow with all the others until finally finishing with the Beatles. I would break up the interviews with sound effects and my voice. This was to be a morsel, a teaser, an invitation to want more, to buy the music paper so as to know more about the these groups.

This was a challenge but I was an old hand. When I had been with the CBC, this was my everyday work.

I had recording tape everywhere and reels hanging on nails. With the tape recorder, I would run the tape slowly over the playback head to hear the exact place to make the edit, then carefully mark the place with a grease pencil. Now the tape was ready to place in the editing block. I would then cut the tape with a razor blade. With the tape still in the editing block, I would finally join two pieces of tape to-

gether by sticking it with the splicing tape. And slowly the
production emerged. This was *Sound of the Stars*.

At last, after six hours of concentration, I was finished.
It was re-recorded and packaged, placed on the next tender
and delivered to Tony Barrow. Soon after that, the country
was flooded with this little disc.

Then at last, two and a half months after our shipwreck,
on April 18th, our dear MV *Mi Amigo* returned to the airwaves with a fifty thousand-watt transmitter, a frequency
of 259 meters, a new jingle package and many other new
improvements. Ronan explained that this was the most
powerful AM transmitter manufactured at that time. We
sang the song "Rule Britannia," but with our own words:

> *Rule the Caroline,*
> *The Caroline rules the waves,*
> *We, never, never, never shall be slaves.*

We had become the true rulers of the seas.

Chapter 10

What is a Nation?

"Satisfaction" by the Rolling Stones was up full blast. I was jumping and dancing to it. The seagulls were keeping a safe distance. We were finally back on the now refurbished, more powerful and newly polished MV *Mi Amigo*. The studio was compact and efficient, with our two cartridge machines for commercials and our two turntables, but just in case the sea once again became too rough and the needle wouldn't stay in the groove, we again taped two large, old English pennies to the top of the pickup for extra weight. Then if that didn't work, we would turn on one of the two reel-to-reel tape recorders. But even on our newly refurbished studio, still the toughest problem was preventing the rumble of the generator from being transmitted through the microphone stand. So once again we hung the microphone from the ceiling and as the ship rolled, we would follow it as we spoke. It was really impossible to be a serious deejay on Radio Caroline.

Out of the corner of my eye I spotted a boat coming toward us, bouncing across the waves. I shouted down to Mike who was enjoying the sun at the stern of our ship. "Hey! A boat's coming."

"Where?" he shouted back.

"Look there!"

"It must be some fishing boat."

"It's the tender!"

"I guess they're bringing food supplies and mail?"

"That's strange!" I said. "We just had a supply boat. A boat isn't due for another two days." I started wondering if something was wrong. The supply boat's schedule was pretty regular. As the small boat drew near, I could see two men in the boat, the skipper at the wheel and someone else. He began to come into focus. It was Ronan. He waved and called out but his words were lost in the wind.

"What the hell? Ronan's onboard!" I said to Mike.

"Let's tell Dave." Climbing the stairs from the sleeping berths was Rosko, rubbing his eyes.

"What's goin' on?" Rosko mumbled.

I pointed, "The tender's coming and Ronan's onboard."

Ronan was still calling to us. Now I could understand. "Tom! We've been invaded! Our tower's been invaded!"

"What tower?" I shouted back.

Now he was waving frantically. "Quick, jump onboard." he shouted. "I'll tell you."

As the tender moved alongside Caroline, I sprang from

Mi Amigo, Radio Caroline South

Caroline to the small craft and landed with a thud. We moved away from Caroline.

I got my footing. "What's this about an invasion? And what tower?"

"The Rough Tower, baby. It became ours because I put a man on it. That was last week."

"So what happened?" I asked in confusion. I had no idea what he was talking about.

"Yesterday, Roy Bates, owner of Radio Essex, invaded our tower and forced our man ashore," Ronan explained.

"That's piracy!" I said. "But what do we need a tower for? Are we going to broadcast from it?"

"Hell no, I'm going to make it into a nation," Ronan said with a sparkle.

"A nation?" I said somewhat amazed. "What the hell for?"

Ronan laughed, then smiling, put his hand on my shoulder. "It's legally possible," he said. "All it needs is a name and a constitution and so on."

Suddenly I understood. "Hey, if you can create a nation, then anyone can create a nation."

"That's right, Tommy baby! The whole concept of na-

Tom spins a request from a listener

tionalism becomes absurd. If people can see that, then one of the causes of war will be eliminated. Great music and art comes from politically unrestricted areas, like out here in international waters."

My imagination began to swirl. What is a nation? A picture emerged of a group of people who decided they were a nation. In fact, a nation doesn't exist until a group of people give it a name, a flag and maybe a constitution, laws or a history. Then the group of people consider themselves as citizens. If a nation is nothing but an idea until someone makes it a reality, then of course Ronan could create one.

A seagull swooped down for some scraps on the ocean surface. My admiration for Ronan was deepening as we headed out to sea in the direction of a mark on the horizon that was getting larger and larger. Slowly I could make it out. There were two towers, each twenty feet in diameter and sixty feet high. A steel platform was across the top of the towers carrying two old, rusty anti-aircraft guns. In the middle of the platform stood a large, two-story structure with windows. On its flat roof was a machine-gun platform. The towers were stained with years of sea and wind. A ladder hung down the side of one of the towers. This was a formidable looking fort. It had been built by the British for defense during World War II but abandoned after the war. Since it was located in international waters, it was available to anyone.

The skipper throttled down as we headed for the ladder, and then suddenly the water was boiling. We all ducked down. We were being fired at by someone with a machine gun. The skipper lost hold of the steering wheel and the boat spun around. The force of the turn sent us hard into the bulkhead. Ronan shouted, "Oh, Holy Mary, Mother of God! Let's get the hell out of here!"

I looked at Ronan, he was hunching down and had turned white, and I was shaking and crouching in the corner.

The skipper grabbed the wheel. The boat surged away. Carefully, I got up and looked back. A small figure was shaking his fist and shouting, and then he started throwing gasoline bombs at us. These hit the water, bursting into flames. One landed onboard. Ronan grabbed the fire extinguisher and, in a cloud of caustic smoke, smothered the fire. I watched the tower as we sped away.

I was still shaking. But Ronan had gained an energy that I had never before seen in him. "Now that's what you would call a close call," he said.

"That guy nearly killed us!" I said, feeling the adrenaline swirling through my body.

"That's for sure. That man is pretty desperate to hold onto that tower."

"How are we going to get the tower back?" I asked with a husky voice.

"Let him have it. We've got a fine ship."

I learned later that Roy Bates created a nation out of that tower and called it Sealand. The last I heard, he is still out there. He has been selling stamps, passports and even has his own currency, a constitution and a history. It also has an offshore Internet hosting facility or "data haven." A number of amateur athletes have represented Sealand in sporting events, but above all, Roy Bates and his son, Michael Bates, are its only citizens. So much for nationalism, I guess.

I climbed back onboard the MV *Mi Amigo* a little

bruised. The news report that night about our adventure was slanted to emphasize that we were unsavory. On the *ITN News* the announcer said, "Men from Radio Caroline tried to land on Rough Tower, a lonely fort seven miles off Harwich, but the tower was already occupied and they were driven off by petrol bombs and shots fired from the tower." They

The Rough Tower

showed shots of the tower and the damage that our tender had suffered.

Then there were scenes of the army preparing to explode the Sunk Head Fort, another World War II fort in the North Sea. Oxy-acetylene cutting equipment was being dropped by helicopter and the newsman reported: "Army prepares to explode Sunk Head Fort to stop it from being used for an offshore radio station."

But to really tarnish our image, they also reported in almost the same breath: "Today, owner of pirate station, Radio City, Reg Calvert was found shot dead. Major Oliver Smedley was accused of the murder. James McKnight and other men invaded Radio City and had refused to leave."

There were also clips from the Postmaster General, Sir Anthony Wedgwood-Benn: "The pirates are a menace and I don't believe, at all, that the public wouldn't support action to enforce the law. The pirate radio ships have no future at all. I'm quite convinced of that!" Radio City was on a fort in the Thames Estuary, nine miles from Whitstable, Kent.

By the spring of 1967, there were ten pirate radio stations broadcasting from the seas, enveloping Great Britain in a wide range of music. Some were on ships and some were on the old World War II ocean defense towers. Radio Caroline's two ships were encouraging anyone who had a few records and the spirit of adventure to create a radio station. The British thirst for pop music and commercial radio was being hammered home to Westminster and Whitehall.

CHAPTER 11

The Bacon
Sandwich Mutiny

We were an easygoing bunch of guys. We played practical jokes on each other or just romped around the deck, climbing the rigging, hanging on the stays and darting up and down the ladders. Shaving soap was fun, the spray can kind. But there was this one captain who was a "Mister Auchtung!" or "Mister Straight-jacket." The moment he arrived onboard he laid down strict rules of behavior, and our antics were not acceptable. Slowly this began to affect the morale of the radio crew and then the sound of our on-air programming.

One morning when I woke for my morning show I was listening to Mike Ahern, who had been doing the all-night show. He was playing Small Faces' "All or Nothing." As I came into the studio I heard him say, "Time to go. This is Mike Ahern saying bye from Radio Caroline. Tom Lodge will be here next."

The sound of his voice had no life. I knew something was wrong. "Morning, Mike."

"Hi."

"What's up, Mike? You look upset."

"I can't do a good show with this Nazi dictatorial captain hanging over my head all the time."

"What happened?"

"He wouldn't let me make a bloody bacon sandwich in the middle of the night. Can you believe that?"

"You're joking!" I said. "I'll talk to the little Hitler."

I was furious. Mike was on-the-air from midnight to 6 a.m. and obviously he would get hungry. When he was hungry, he would put on a long cut from an LP and make a sandwich in the kitchen galley. I went running up to the bridge where our Dutch captain was checking the charts and dials. "Captain, my staff can't work with you hanging over their heads like this all the time."

"I am zee Captain of zis ship. I demand obedience," he shot back without looking up.

"The morale of the radio staff is paramount to our jobs. Without the radio station, you're out of a job!"

But he did not want to hear it. "You don't tell me about morale," he yelled. "I run zis ship. Zis is my bridge." He pointed to the door. "You get off my bridge!"

I became even more angry. "Now you've gone too far!" I said as I left the bridge.

Later, when the captain was having his afternoon nap, I went on the radiophone and put in a call. "Ronan," I insisted, "This can't go on. The deejays are all upset. We've got to get rid of this captain!"

"That's mutiny, Tom," he joked. "Calm down. Don't worry. You go on with your show."

"Mutiny or not, he has to go!"

"What's really happening, Tom?"

"He's running the ship as if it were a military operation," I explained, calming down a bit. "It's as if we were soldiers under his command. And all the guys are upset. Ronan, the whole morale of the ship is zero and it is effecting the programming. I tell you, it's showing on-the-air. The spark has gone out! The guys have lost their spontaneity, their enthusiasm and their fun. We are not sounding as good as we should or can." I was getting upset again, "Ronan, there is no question here. Either he goes or we will definitely lose out to Radio London."

"Tommy baby, calm down! What's he doing?"

"It's yes sir, no sir, three bags full sir! Look, last night while Mike was doing the all-night show, he went to make a sandwich and the captain gave him hell. He said he couldn't do that; he couldn't help himself to make a sandwich. Ronan, Mike was very upset, he was hungry and needed to eat. Since he couldn't eat, the rest of his show was dreary. The captain has to go, Ronan. He is an auchtung sergeant with everyone. Please, Ronan, do something!"

"Okay, I'll take care of it. Tell the guys not to worry. Just hang in there. Okay then, talk to you soon."

"Thanks, Ronan. Bye."

Just as I finished, the captain walked in. I left without speaking to him. I don't know if he heard. I didn't care.

The next day the tender arrived. There was a stranger onboard. He climbed over the side and onboard. We were all on deck along with the ship's crew and the captain. The stranger settled his footing on the moving deck and, with a big smile and a strong Dutch accent, he announced, "I'm your new captain." He stepped forward and handed Captain "Auchtung" an envelope.

We all stood with our mouths open. The Dutch crew was dumbfounded. I heard the word mutiny and I realized what I had done *was* mutiny—because at sea, the captain is king.

"Very well," said our old captain. "You can takeover zis damn floating-junk jukebox that's full of riff-raff. I'm glad to be leaving here!" He went up to his cabin, grabbed his belongings and left.

Our new captain climbed up to the bridge and immediately took over the ship. As soon as the tender had left with Captain Auchtung, we all jumped in the air and screamed with relief. We started frantically chasing each other around the deck. We were barking like dogs and making jungle noises.

DLT came to attention and imitated our departed old captain, "Stop zis! You will go straight to your cabins! Now!"

Someone blew a raspberry at DLT. He looked disappointed, turned around and walked off. He had a tail attached to his bottom. Everyone burst out laughing and DLT shook his tail.

Once again the radio programming became fun and life on our little tub became a joy. The fan mail soon tripled. We were moving into the stratosphere of popularity.

On my next shore leave I walked into Ronan's office, and there was Ronan laughing. In fact, he was laughing from the bottom of his socks. "What's so funny?" I asked.

"Oh, you'll never guess, Tommy baby." He had to catch his breath. "This place is nuts!"

"What happened?"

"Well, we've been trying to get the Pepsi-Cola account for some time now and I had an appointment with Joan Crawford."

"The actress?"

"Yes, she's on their board." He started to laugh again. "Oh, this is too much. Boy, what a joke."

"What happened?" I persisted.

"Anyway, it was all set up for this afternoon. So first I kept her waiting. Well, this is England, you know. You have to keep people waiting. Then I set the scene. I had a bottle of pop with a straw in it and I placed the other end of the straw here in John Kennedy's mouth,"

Still laughing, he pointed to the bronze head of JFK, "It looked fantastic. I mean, there was the top American sucking on the best American drink. Sounds good, doesn't it?" he said looking at me.

"Yes," I said, "that sounds perfect."

"So here's the scene. Joan Crawford is shown into the office. She walks in with the grandeur of a movie star, her clothes flowing behind her. I get up to greet her. She walks in like a princess from antiquity. She sees the bust of Kennedy. She suddenly stops short. Gasps! And then turns around and, with her head held high, she walks out."

"What? That's terrible. What happened?"

"You know what I had done, Tommy baby? That bottle of pop that I had placed for Kennedy to drink from was not

Mealtime on Radio Caroline South

Pepsi-Cola, her company. No, it was Coca-Cola." Again he started to laugh, and this time I joined him.

Despite losing the Pepsi-Cola account, things were good. Our popularity was exploding. The survey that was done in August 1966 indicated we had an audience of 23 million listeners. We took out a magazine ad with the head-line, "23 Million Listeners Can't Be Wrong!"

There were continuous visits from newspaper journal-ists, magazine journalists and TV interviewers. Now when we went ashore, we were always recognized.

Then there was that one memorable morning. I was playing the Troggs' "With a Girl Like You" and the music was on full blast, filling the whole studio. The record came to an end. "That's one of my fave groups," I said. "This is the sound that Radio Caroline is all about. And here's a request going out to Julie. Thanks for the Mars Bar, I love Mars Bars. In fact, they are my favorite chocolate bar. So while I'm eating this, here's your song, Manfred Mann and

'Pretty Flamingo.'" I started the disc. The show went on and I thought no more about it. It was nothing out of the ordinary, just another fun show.

In a few days the tender brought our supplies and mail; I was swamped with packages. I mean thousands, yes, thousands of packages. I had no idea what this was all about. I dragged the mailbags into the lounge and began opening the packages. Each one contained a Mars Bar. Each one was responding to my simple words, "I love Mars Bars." It became very clear that when you have millions and millions of listeners, you better be careful what you say and do because the response will be multiplied many times.

To improve advertising sales, Ronan hired two first-class radio-air salesmen from Edmonton, Alberta, Canada. They were "hot." We called them Batman and Robin. Their real names were Allan Slaight and Terry Bates. They were true go-getters. We English can be a little too proper and sometimes a little slow. But these two guys were fast, which is why we named them after the original Dynamic Duo.

They created a great sales contest called Caroline Cash Casino. It was a contest wherein prize money increased with each wrong answer. Starting at £100, it quickly grew into the thousands. One winner received £4,070.

The announcer of the contest was Bill Hearne, a Canadian radioman whose enthusiasm gave the contest that extra something. The listener would mail in a box top from one of the breakfast cereal advertisers along with a ten-shilling note and their answer to the current question. We would open the letters on-the-air and with each wrong answer the prize money would increase. I remember going into Caroline House on one of my shore leaves and finding the reception area, the halls and even the basement overflowing with mailbags. Each letter contained a ten-shilling note. Yes, we had hit the jackpot!

It felt powerful to have these two salesmen bringing in the advertising. Even though Anthony Wedgwood-Benn was determined to get us off-the-air—and later Edward Short, who drafted a bill for this purpose—there was a feeling on both ships, and in Caroline House, that we were invincible.

Everywhere you turned, people were benefiting from Radio Caroline. For many, it was a springboard into a successful business. Richard Branson, at 16 years old, had been a student running his school paper when we started. He used the student paper to create a mail order service for the records we would play that were not widely available in the stores. Soon he made deals with American record companies to get their songs played on Radio Caroline. He made his big move when he opened a record store on Oxford Street in London and called it Virgin Records. Then there was Allan Slaight, who went from being our on-the-air radio salesman to one of Canada's top communication moguls. He now owns Standard Broadcasting in Canada.

The established record companies also took advantage of the vast exposure Caroline could give them in the UK. Decca created a new label, Deram, and RCA launched Vertigo and Neon. Smaller record companies also enjoyed new success. Pye Records started in the UK in 1953, and had among their artists the Kinks and the Searchers. Chris

Blackwell's Island Records flourished after he moved it from Jamaica to England in 1962.

Many other labels were launched at this time. The Rolling Stones' manager, Andrew Loog Oldham, founded Immediate Records. Reaction Records only lasted two years, but counted among its artists the Who and Cream. Kit Lambert and Chris Stamp, managers of the Who, created Track Records in 1967 and signed the Jimi Hendrix Experience, The Who, and The Parliaments. Other small labels included Karma Sutra, Page One, Regal Zonophone, established in 1932 and then revived in 1967, and Major Minor, founded by Phil Solomon.

And then, of course, there were all the bands and musicians who would never have broken through if they had to rely on the BBC Light Programme for exposure: the Yardbirds, the Kinks, the Who, Cilla Black, the Troggs, Them, the Animals, Tom Jones, the Zombies, Manfred Mann, and on and on.

1966: Tom with Jeanine and (*l to r*) Lionel, Tommy, Brodie

Carnaby Street was the fashion industry's Radio Caroline; Mary Quant and others rode this wave and filled our desire for continually new, colorful and exciting clothes. And make no mistake, it was the music that led to Carnaby! Yes, the music was the foundation of a powerhouse that knocked down the barriers of English conservatism. This outpouring of euphoric energy was most disturbing to the comfortable and well-established English elders. Finding a way to stop us became essential in order to maintain their security. The question was how to close us down and still maintain political support from the people.

The battle was heating up. In the August 6, 1966 issue of *Disc and Music Echo*, George Harrison said in an interview with Ray Colman: "I can't understand the Government's attitude over the pirates. Why don't they make the BBC illegal as well—it doesn't give the public the service it wants. Otherwise the pirates wouldn't be here to fill the gap. The Government makes me sick. This is becoming a police state. They should leave the 'pirates' alone. At least they've had a go, which is more than the BBC has done."

CHAPTER 12

Armed with
Rock and Roll

I was lying on my bunk reading through a vast pile of fan mail. On-the-air was "Here Comes the Night" by Them. The sea was relatively calm and I was content. Yes, life was good.

For no particular reason, I glanced out the porthole. Imagine my surprise when I noticed what looked to be the entire British fleet headed right for us. I jumped up and stuck my head out the porthole to get a better view. Several large, gray ships sitting high in the water were moving fast with white foam spraying up from their bows. They were just like the battleships from the movies, but also from my early childhood. Memories of being four and sailing away from Europe after Hitler invaded France in World War II came back to me. A German U-boat sunk the passenger ship in front of the ship that carried me and my family. To protect us, escorting British naval ships surrounded us and covered us with a smokescreen. I was scared then and just like being a child again, I was scared now. They were coming to sink Radio Caroline. Each ship was flying the Union Jack and their bows were sharp and menacing with guns pointed in our direction. I rushed up the stairs from the cabins and headed directly to the studio. DLT was on-the-air.

"Quick, Dave. Look out the porthole!"

"Why? What's happening?" Dave peered through the port-hole. "Hey, that's something! They're heading right for us!"

"It's the British Royal Navy!" I said.

"That's a drag! What're we gonna do?"

"Here's what we do," I said. "We'll talk about them on-the-air, okay? That'll make their actions public imme-diately. If they step out of line, the public will hear about it on the radio, right now. All we have to do is send them some record dedications and some friendly words. Quick now, Dave!"

Dave interrupted the record that was playing. While he was speaking he found another record in one of the boxes and placed the needle on the record.

"This is Dave Lee Travis on Radio Caroline South," he said. "I don't know what's going on, but there is a large fleet of Royal Navy ships heading right towards us. Hello, you sailors out there. The next song is dedicated to you and it's the Rolling Stones with '19th Nervous Breakdown.'"

"I'll get the ships' names," I said as I ran to get a pair of binoculars. The other deejays came into the studio to see what was going on. Out on the deck I stared across the wa-ter, picking out the names.

I shouted to Dave through the porthole. "There's HMS *Invincible!*"

Dave immediately sent the info out on-the-air. "Hello, HMS *Invincible*. If you're listening to us, flash us with your lights."

"I see another one," I said. "HMS *Arrow*, HMS *Hermes* and HMS *Sheffield*. They are still heading toward us!"

Dave kept broadcasting, "We are also having a visit from HMS *Arrow* and HMS *Hermes* of the Royal Navy. Hello, you sailors! If you're listening to us, flash us with your lights. My next song is dedicated to the fleet of Her Majesty's Royal Navy, which is heading straight toward us!" Full blast over the speakers came "Wild Thing" by the Troggs.

Millions of listeners were absorbed in the excitement. I learned later that many people stopped their work and crowded around a radio. This was a true British drama on the high seas. This was another Spanish Armada. Our radio was our gun. We kept sending dedications to the sailors. We kept inviting them to communicate with us by flashing lights. But there was no response. Then a strange thing happened. Suddenly, and without any signal, they all turned 180 degrees and sailed away.

"They're going," I said. "Wow! That was a close one!"

Dave broke into the record that was playing, "Somebody Help Me" by the Spencer Davis Group, and said, "The ships are turning around. It looks like they're leaving. From Radio Caroline, we wish the Royal Navy bon voyage. And hey, you sailors on the British Royal Navy ships, we'll give you all free tickets to our next rock and roll concert that we're going to be throwing real soon. And just to say thanks for the visit, here are the Kinks with 'Sunny Afternoon.'"

"Wow, that was something!" said Dave to me off-air. "I guess they decided that broadcasting their whereabouts wasn't good for their Royal image. Yeah, we got 'em good, didn't we?"

Just then the captain came through the studio door. "We just received a message that our Panama Registration has been canceled."

"What do we do now?" I asked.

"Come on deck and I'll show you," he replied.

We followed the captain out on deck to the mast where our flag was flying. He pulled down the Panama flag. As he was pulling hand over hand he said, "Ronan had a lot of foresight. We've got another nine flags ready to go. Each from different countries, just in case something happens."

"That's clever," I said.

The captain unfolded a new flag, a Honduras flag. "Hey, that's a pretty flag," I said. "The color matches my shirt. Good old Honduras, now we're still legal. Great!" We all cheered. The captain turned and looked toward the shore. We followed his gaze. There was a small craft approaching. It was loaded with sightseers for "A Trip Around Radio Caroline."

The captain laughed, "Hey guys, because they can't come onboard, give them a fun show." We waved, threw kisses and climbed the rigging. The skipper of the small craft threw a package of requests onboard and then headed back to shore.

Shortly after our encounter with the Royal Navy I was

Ronan and
the the flag of
Honduras

standing on the stern deck of Radio Caroline, listening to
our broadcast, when it suddenly hit me! Something extraordinary was happening here. Yes, Caroline was important
and unusual, playing rock and roll to a nation that had been
deprived and isolated from it. But how did it all get started?
Where did this amazing music come from?

I remembered when I was eighteen and living in Canada; I had never heard such sounds. A year later, in 1955,
while I was traveling on a bus through West Virginia down
to my childhood land of Virginia, I heard a new sound on
the radio from a new singer called Elvis. He was singing
"Blue Moon of Kentucky." I was enthralled.

Later, in Raleigh, North Carolina, I was driving a tractor
on my godfather's daffodil farm, tilling the rows between
the bulbs. I went to see a movie, *Blackboard Jungle*, with its
theme of "Rock Around the Clock." Rock and roll had pene-
trated my heart. I was exited. As I drove the tractor the next
day I could hardly contain this new raw energy, this new
life, this new feeling deep in my body. I drove the tractor
up and down the rows, passing other people working in the
field, including a pretty black girl working between the rows.

Passing time on a sunny afternoon

That evening I searched the radio airwaves for more rock and roll, the whole time fantasizing about that girl. Her slender, shapely legs and the smooth curves of her face surrounding those large brown eyes and the most kissable lips I had ever seen; the whole time her sensuality kept intermingling in my mind with the sounds I was hearing of rock and roll. She wore a loose, shabby dress that made her body more enticing. But it was the color of her skin that touched my deep sexuality. Of course, I never spoke to her. In 1955 Virginia, segregation was still paramount and there could have been consequences for either one of us.

But even then rock and roll was beginning to help wash away some of those racial barriers, those walls of protection. The white music on the American music charts was influenced by the black rhythms, intonations and instrumentations.

It was an amazing musical journey that had begun a tidal wave of energy. It occurred to me that, with Radio Caroline and Pirate Radio, we now had three separate waves of radio that fed this music transformation.

The first wave occurred in 1951 when Alan Freed introduced the music he named rock 'n' roll, black slang for making love. He introduced the music of the African Americans from Radio WJW in Cleveland and organized the first rock 'n' roll concert at Cleveland Arena on March 21st in 1952. It ended in a riot. Not only did he create the concept of rock 'n' roll, he created another concept, the "teenager," a word

Tom, sorting mail with Rosko and Rick Dane

Tourists would often cruise out to look at Caroline. Sometimes they would come along side and pass up requests to the crew.

never used before then. His popularity took him to Radio WINS in New York City, which he turned into a rock 'n' roll station, bringing the music to a wider audience.

The next wave came when Sam Phillips, creator of Sun Records, discovered and launched the music of Rufus Thomas, B.B. King and Howlin' Wolf. Later he would break through the racial barriers in music with Elvis Presley, Johnny Cash, Jerry Lee Lewis, Roy Orbison, Conway Twitty, Charlie Rich and Carl Perkins. All of these artists were white. "I always knew that the rebellion of young people, which is as natural as breathing, would be part of that breakthrough," Perkins would later say. The Elvis hits of "Heartbreak Hotel," "Hound Dog" and "Don't be Cruel" pushed the new sound deep into the heart of white America.

And now Radio Caroline was creating the third wave of radio, broadcasting a raw, energetic music that only a few British youths were playing and recording. They had been influenced by the records that they had discovered, that they had copied—and then changed to their own style—from a few carefully gathered records that they had collected, mostly from American sailors who had visited this island. Yes, the rebellion of young people was part of this breakthrough, too—this change from the safe pop of Guy Mitchell's "Heartaches by the Number" to the Rolling Stones' "Get Off of My Cloud."

When Sam Phillips created the records for the music of the second wave of radio, he saw that the American teenagers had no music of their own. On Radio Caroline, we too saw that the British teenagers had no music of their own. This third wave of radio was opening the door to musical freedom. Britain was full of undiscovered talent, which we were most fortunate to have available to broadcast from our ship.

We had created a channel through which all this youthful, creative talent could be expressed. First it was the music: the Rolling Stones, the Who, the Yardbirds, the Kinks, the Animals, and on and on. Then fashion and art followed. The combination made a creative, alternative way of life acceptable. Once the British public was exposed to all this new expression, their pent up energy exploded in a continual flowering of color and fun.

This third wave was not only transforming the British nation, but was surging back across the Atlantic. The "British Invasion of America" revitalized the American teenagers of the '60s and into the '70s. Music was the great international communicator, spreading freedom and life to all that were ready to hear.

That evening, standing on the stern deck of Radio Caroline, I suddenly let out a huge holler of great joy. Life was exhilarating!

CHAPTER 13

The Shirt Off My Back

It was September 1966 and I had just returned home for my one-week shore leave. Jeanine and the boys were tanned from a great summer of sunshine. The boys took me around and showed me a fort that they had built behind our house. They were pirates on the high seas and the field was the ocean. Jeanine had a special French meal and wine for us. And after much excitement, fun and love, I dropped off to sleep with the Troggs' hit song, "With a Girl Like You," playing in my head.

The next morning was Sunday and we all had a lie in, staying in bed until the sun shining through the window and our yearning for pancakes and orange juice pulled us out of our beds. The phone interrupted the quiet. I was being called up to London to emcee a gig. When I think back to that day, I have no recollection as to who the bands were.

Tom with Fans

I am sure that they were not very big. But that is not the main point of the story.

I remember asking Jeanine, "Could you make me a special outfit for the gig?"

"What do you have in mind?"

"Something more flamboyant than Carnaby Street," I said.

She laughed, "Don't be silly." Then after a moment she continued, "But I'll see what I can do."

Jeanine made me this impressive satin turquoise shirt with full, puffy sleeves, lace on the cuffs and a flounce along the bottom. The collar had a white braid sown on in a wavy pattern. It was gorgeous. The pants were aquamarine and blue satin. They were tight on the thighs and came with bell-bottoms. I dug out a pair of blue shoes with large gold buckles. Impressive! Now I was ready to prance across any stage.

A friend came to look after the boys and then Jeanine and I drove off in our Triumph with sandwiches and all my special gear for the concert.

Driving through the English countryside was always a pleasure; the different shades of green, the old oak trees, the stonewalled fields with sheep, the little streams winding by old mills and the thousand-year-old villages. Car radios were still not a common feature in the UK, so as we rode along we sang the Kinks' hit, "Sunny Afternoon:"

Help me, help me, help me sail away,
Well give me two good reasons why I oughta stay.
'Cause I love to live so pleasantly,
Live this life of luxury,
Lazing on a sunny afternoon.

We had been booked into a comfortable hotel around the corner from the venue. Jeanine helped me dress and made a few last minute alterations. She looked at me approvingly and kissed me deeply.

I donned a coat and dark glasses and we slipped unnoticed out of the hotel, down the street and then in the backstage door. The band was setting up and the audience was arriving. I peeked through an opening in the curtain. The place was swimming with high-energy teenagers, chatting, running here and there, and calling out to their friends. This is going to be a good concert, I thought.

The moment came. I ran out on stage, grabbed the microphone and the audience screamed.

"This is Radio Caroline bringing you the finest rock and roll!" I shouted. The audience cheered again.

Then one girl in the front grabbed my ankle and pulled. I fell forward onto a group of girls clustered at the first few rows. They screamed as I collapsed into the middle of them.

Then many hands pulled on my shirt, grabbing in all directions. I could hear it rip. As it tore, they pulled harder and harder and suddenly it came right off of my back in a few jagged pieces. I scrambled, topless, back onstage and watched with amazement as this group of girls tore my shirt into many pieces. Each one wanted a Tom Lodge souvenir. How could love be so violent?

I was undeterred, however. Bare-chested, I shouted into the microphone, "Do you want more?"

"Yes!" they shouted back.

"Are you ready to go all the way?"

"Yes!" they shouted.

"Alright then, here's the band, now go total!" The band crashed in with their first chord and I ran off stage. Jeanine was waiting for me.

"Wow!" I said

Jeanine said, "They destroyed such a beautiful shirt. How weird."

Tom on stage

"Yes," I said. "It's sure dangerous out there."

Someone lent me a shirt and I finished the concert with no more personal drama.

After the concert, Jeanine and I found a quiet, romantic restaurant where I slowly was able to wind down. After having our fill of warm food and soothing red wine, we escaped back to our hotel.

All these adventures on and off the ship, with both the ups and the downs, were bringing Jeanine and I closer and closer together. Nothing could deaden our spirits.

CHAPTER 14

A Pirate's Progress

We were becoming more and more vibrant and the government was becoming more and more antagonistic. We were promoting concerts all over the country, encouraging musicians to wear flamboyant clothes, to make their music bold and innovative. Above all, we were infusing the freedom to be daring and wild into the cultural fabric.

The government was resorting to every stunt it could dream up to close us down. In response we answered on-air, the government's continuous onslaught against us. They would go on television and say that we were a menace to shipping. We explained that we were anchored far way from shipping routes. They said that we were breaking the laws. We pointed out that since we were beyond the three-mile limit, we were in international waters and in total compliance with internationally agreed on laws of the sea.

From the onslaught of letters of support we received, the idea slowly emerged to have a parade to support commercial radio. The city of Ilford, Essex, an eastern suburb of Greater London, was delighted for us to do this and the people of Essex were eager to create it. We received letters from Ilford businesses supporting the idea of a parade. Since the parade would be broadcast on Radio Caroline, it would assist their businesses by bringing tourists and exposure. The enthusiasm to support Radio Caroline and the other offshore radio stations brought thousands of people together. They built impressively decorated floats with dancing girls and, local bands appeared. Deejays Robbie Dale and Graham Webb were there throughout the celebrations, blaring rock and roll into the streets and homes of Ilford.

I was on-air and gave the event maximum exposure as well. The support for Radio Caroline was so high that people from all over the country were doing whatever they could to keep us from being taken off-the-air by Anthony Wedgwood-Benn and the government.

That evening on the ship I watched the *ITN News*. They showed floats all covered in flowers and decorations built in the shapes of our ships. Bikini-dressed girls wearing captain caps and pirate hats waved flags with pictures of our ship or of skull and crossbones. They were dancing to our music. The streets were lined with young people, old people, mothers and their children, people with short hair and long hair. It appeared as if every strata of society was there to have a party and to declare, "We want the pirates!"

Then on one of the floats I saw Robbie waving to the crowds with Graham. I switched the TV to the BBC channel and to my surprise, they too were covering the parade. We could not have dreamed of such total support and so much enthusiasm. The event was a huge success, beyond what we imagined.

We didn't need a parade however, to let us know how popular we had become. The reaction was evident at the concerts we hosted and the promotional events we attended. I was almost always recognized by somebody whenever I was ashore.

Despite our growing popularity, in reality, we were only observers of the music scene. After a brief moment, it was time to return to the ship and the music.

I was always comfortable at Caroline House. It was our foundation. But even there I was only visiting. It was during one of my trips to Caroline House back in the spring of 1965 that I was introduced to Eric Clapton, the young guitar player of the Yardbirds. I offered him some tea.

"Eric, I think 'For Your Love' is great. I've been giving it lots of play. I love it."

"Well, I don't," he replied.

"Really? Why?"

"It's too poppy. I'm a bluesman. I've left the Yardbirds and am joinin' John Mayall's Bluesbreakers."

This was not what I had expected. "You've left the Yardbirds? I didn't know that. That's a great shame, a hard line for the band. So who's taken your place then?"

He shrugged. "They wanted Jimmy."

"Jimmy?"

"Jimmy Page. He's not going to do it. He's whole-time in the studio, probably making a packet."

"Who then?"

"Jimmy's mate, Jeff Beck. He's alright."

"Oh." There wasn't much more to say. I shook his hand. "Right, then. Good luck to you."

Clapton nodded, turned and left. I wasn't sure what would happen to him.

The Yardbirds continued to make good music with Jeff Beck. "Heart Full of Soul" was a big hit in the UK and the US. It probably only missed being a number one hit because of another song that became a favorite: the Hollies' "I'm Alive." Later on, I often played the Yardbirds' "Shapes of Things" and "Over Under Sideways Down."

After leaving the Yardbirds, Jeff Beck broke into the UK charts with a solo hit, "Hi-Ho Silver Lining." Although maybe not as commercially successful as some of the other artists, his reputation as a giant among guitarists has only grown over the years.

Jimmy Page finally decided to leave the studio and join Beck in the Yardbirds. Later, his attempt to have a "New Yardbirds" with Robert Plant, John Bonham and John Paul Jones became a much larger sensation—Led Zeppelin.

I remembered my conversation with Eric Clapton when, back on Caroline in late 1966, we received a copy of a record from a new band, Cream, which Clapton had formed with Jack Bruce and Ginger Baker. We gave one tune, "I Feel Free," some good play and it had a little success in the UK. But it was only the beginning of his legendary career.

Out on the ship though, we really didn't have time for the coming and goings of the musicians. And we were, for the most part, out of the reach of industry executives, producers and managers.

We were free to be alone with the music and uninhibited about sharing what we liked with the eager public. My taste in music was completely open for everybody to hear and either enjoy or criticize.

On Caroline there were no outside influences, no telephones and no business control. We were fortunate to be surrounded by the continual rolling seas. We were definitely a force within the music business, but we had no idea of this. And the music was always changing. We offered airtime to the musicians and they, in turn, became more and more creative and inventive.

As program director, I gave the deejays full freedom to

In the studio, 1967

play the records that they liked and avoid the records that they did not like. It was this freedom that was the thrust of our success on Radio Caroline. Each deejay's show had its own style. They had their own favorites and they also had the records that they would not play.

Take January 1966 as an example. None of us played Petula Clark's "You're The One," Ken Dodd's "The River" or Cliff Richard's "Wind Me Up," even though these all made the top twenty charts.

Then there were the records that I did not play but some of the others did. Dave Lee Travis played the Shadows' "War Lord," a song I wouldn't touch. Robbie Dale liked Gerry and the Pacemakers' "Walk Hand in Hand"— but not me. Mike Ahern played Andy Williams' "Do You Hear What I Hear" but that song was never heard on the *Tom Lodge Show*.

Of course, there were other records that I liked so much I would give them an extra push. I would spend extra time talking about the band and their new song. Good examples of this were songs like "My Generation" by the Who, "Like a Rolling Stone" by Bob Dylan, "It's My Life" by the Animals, and my favorite, "Walk Like a Man" by the Four Seasons. For a while, a constant feature on my show was "Hang on Sloopy" by the McCoys.

The Four Seasons were a special case. They were right up there with the most played groups on my shows. Dave, Mike and Robbie would needle me about this every chance they got. In fact, I'm not sure anybody ever understood my attraction. I enjoyed the harmony and the falsetto voice. I loved "Let's Hang On," "Rag Doll" and "Silence is Golden" (the B-side of "Rag Doll"). I played this song so many times, starting in 1964, that I'm sure I helped influence this being covered by the Tremeloes. They had a number two hit with the song in May 1967.

In April 1964, when I first joined Radio Caroline, the Beatles' "She Loves You" had recently been number one. I didn't care for it. I recognized their talent but to me it was too formulaic, a sloppy love song. In that same vein was the Bachelors' "I Believe," Billy J. Kramer & the Dakotas' "Little Children," which I really disliked, and Peter & Gordon's "World Without Love."

At the same time, however, there was the Rolling Stones with one of my favorite songs, "Not Fade Away," the Dave Clark Five's "Bits and Pieces" and the Swinging Blue Jeans with "Good Golly Miss Molly." There was plenty of variety.

I was sometimes partial to a song that even I was surprised I enjoyed. A good example was Millie with "My Boy Lollipop." I guess it's because it had life.

Some slower songs I liked were "Walk on By" by Dionne Warwick and "It's Over" by Roy Orbison. The country hit "I Love You Because," by Jim Reeves, reminded me of my days in Virginia. Almost all my early guitar playing was country. Tom Jones came along with "It's Not Unusual." It was the first of many big hits.

By the summer of 1964 I could really notice that R&B had taken hold. The best example was "House of the Rising Sun" with that rolling blues sound of Alan Price's organ. Its power attracted me like a moth to a light.

It was clear that we were breaking away from the established formula song. The Beatles changed and had a num-

ber one hit with "A Hard Days Night." There was the Nash-
ville Teens with "Tobacco Road," the Beach Boys had their
first hit in the UK with "I Get Around" and the Kinks entered the scene with "You Really Got Me." Now there was
a new feeling in the songs, these were songs that emerged
from people's feelings, not just from some established song
formula—at least that was how it felt to me.

When we first got a copy of Roy Orbison's "Pretty Woman," everyone on Caroline North loved it and sure enough,
by October it was number one.

Some slow ballads and love songs were impossible to
ignore. I loved the Righteous Brothers soulful "You've Lost
That Loving Feelin'," which was the number one hit of Feb-
ruary 1965, and the Kinks did it again with "Tired of Waiting for You." But then the Stones sped it up again with "The
Last Time."

I was always enthusiastic whenever a new record of Bob
Dylan's arrived. We played "Times They Are a-Changin'"
and "Subterranean Homesick Blues" in Spring of 1965, and
later that year we began to spin "Like a Rolling Stone." In
1966 came "Rainy Day Women #12 & 35" and "I Want You."
It is interesting that Dylan had 6 hits in the UK between '65
and '66 while only having 3 hits in the US during that same
period.

The spring and summer of 1966 saw some great music.
The Hollies had another big song with "Bus Stop," as did
the Kinks with their number one hit "Sunny Afternoon."
Manfred Mann also had a number one hit with "Pretty Fla-
mingo." Dusty Springfield had her biggest success with
"You Don't Have to Say You Love Me." Small Faces had a

number one UK hit with "All or Nothing," though it never even made the US charts.

When I first listened to the Troggs earlier in 1966 with "Wild Thing," I knew it would be a big hit. This was followed by "With a Girl Like You," which became a number one in the UK.

Our tender began to deliver more and more music from the States. The variety was incredible with some beautiful tunes. There was Simon and Garfunkel's "Homeward Bound," "Monday, Monday" by the Mamas and the Papas as well as "Daydream" and "Summer in the City" by the Lovin' Spoonful.

We became exposed to more Motown, too. We all loved the records. We didn't exactly know them as Motown songs at first. They were originally released in England on State-

Daydreaming

side Records. The Americans called it soul music and it's easy for me to understand why. The Supremes had always been popular with tunes like "Baby Love" and "Stop! In the Name of Love." Now they released "You Can't Hurry Love" and "You Keep Me Hangin' On." Although not as popular as in the US, they were still high on the charts. The Four Tops, however, did reach the top in the UK as well as the US with "Reach Out I'll Be There."

And the Beatles? They were still a force. They started 1966 with "Day Tripper," a huge hit. A few months after my interview with them, "Day Tripper" was the top song in the US and high in the UK. In August, their album *Revolver* was released and with it came the hits "Yellow Submarine" and "Eleanor Rigby."

Many of our other old friends were still turning out some great music. The Stones had "Paint it Black" and "Have You Seen Your Mother, Baby, Standing in the Shadow?" The Hollies had a big song in the last part of the year with "Stop! Stop! Stop!" The Kinks ended the year with "Dead End Street."

Other countries were joining the party, too. I'm not sure on Caroline whether we even realized it at the time. We liked a song from the Easybeats called "Friday on My Mind." They were from Australia. An even larger success was the song "Black is Black" by Los Bravos. They were from Spain.

Even though the Beach Boys already had three popular songs in 1966, when we first heard "Good Vibrations" we knew it was different. We played it often. I was fascinated by the way Brian Wilson had interwoven the harmony of the voices and the unique instrumentation. Something new was definitely in the air.

If I were to choose a song or two to exemplify the changes in the music that we began to play in 1967, there would be a number of candidates. Maybe it would be something by Donovan, a folk artist who had the popular song "Catch the Wind" in 1965, but nothing since. Now within a few months in early '67 he had "Sunshine Superman," with it's lyrics of "blow your little mind," and then the song "Mellow Yellow."

Perhaps a contender would be a release from a new group, Procol Harum. I first took note of the unusual name, but once I listened to "A Whiter Shade of Pale," I knew there was no denying the power of the song. I couldn't wait to share it with my audience.

For influence, nobody could top the Beatles, really. Everyone on Caroline was amazed at their continual inventiveness, with the use of Eastern sources, cutting-edge lyrics and innovative instrumentation. Of course, this is the year of the *Sgt. Pepper* album, which changed the way we all looked at the LP, but they previewed that sound with "Penny Lane" and "Strawberry Fields."

The name Jimi Hendrix had been around England for a little while, but when I first heard "Hey Joe," I was stunned by the almost supernatural force of his guitar. We loved him. That first song of his, however, didn't even make a dent in the US charts, and although "Purple Haze" did manage to break the Top 100 in the US, we made it a much bigger hit in the UK. Before too long, Hendrix had another song on the British charts with "The Wind Cries Mary."

The Rolling Stones never seemed to let up and I contin-

Kung Fu Tom Lodge

ued to give them lots of airtime. They scored big with "Let's Spend the Night Together" and "Ruby Tuesday."

Some familiar artists just seemed to have created a slightly different sound. The Hollies continued to be popular on Caroline with "On a Carousel" and "Carrie Anne." The Kinks' "Waterloo Sunset" and "Autumn Almanac" were both big in the UK but never took off in the States. The Who had a big year with "Happy Jack," "Pictures of Lily" and "I Can See For Miles."

1967 also saw a new group emerge that had a fairly big song in England with "See Emily Play," but it wasn't heard often in America for quite some time. Their name was Pink Floyd.

There was still plenty of music that was just plain good. Motown was still popular on the ship. In succession, the Four Tops had "Standing in Shadows of Love," "Bernadette" and the unusual sound of "7 Rooms of Gloom" on the charts. And the Supremes had strong hits with "The Happening" and "Reflections." Then a new artist from Motown appeared: Stevie Wonder. The harmonica on "I Was Made to Love Her" made me bounce around Caroline's studio.

My tastes were not infallible, however. While I did play "Dedicated to the One I Love" by the Mamas and Papas, which climbed to the top of the charts, I refused to play "Georgie Girl" by the Seekers and "The Last Waltz" by Engelbert Humperdinck, and they became hits anyway.

For the most part the sound and the lyrics of much of what we were playing had clearly changed. As long as the spirit of freedom was in the song, however, we didn't pay much attention to how the culture was changing. When the

Young Rascals, an American band, released "Groovin'," one line in particular stuck with me: "I can't imagine anything that's better…"

1967 was the year of San Francisco's Summer of Love. Scott McKenzie's "San Francisco (Be Sure to Wear Flowers in Your Hair)" was a huge hit in England, even bigger than in the US. He wasn't alone. A group called the Flower Pot Men had a hit in the UK with "(Let's Go To) San Francisco," and the Animals sang about "San Francisco Nights." We never did see San Francisco, even though we made the music popular.

Were we followers of the changing culture or instigators? A little of both, I think. We didn't have enough time on shore to even notice the emerging drug scene. On Caroline we had a ration of one beer a day.

When the Small Faces sang about "getting high" in their song "Itchycoo Park," I probably knew less about what they were singing than the typical British government official. Yet if I had known something about it, it wouldn't have made any difference. If I liked it, I played it. I had the freedom to spin a new sound if I wanted and the listeners of Radio Caroline had the freedom to enjoy.

CHAPTER 15

This Too Shall Pass

Each time I went ashore it seemed like England had become more colorful. The girls were in miniskirts. The guys were in bell-bottoms. And, of course, there was music everywhere. Romance was in the air, no doubt fueled by the fact that the pill was no longer restricted to only married women. We were the baby-boomers. We were dominant and we were confident. Carnaby Street was abuzz and the King's Road was hip.

This particular shore leave I was walking down the King's Road and was attracted by the vibrant clothes in a new boutique. They were unique in both design and color. I walked in. A striking girl with stylishly-cut hair came forward. "Hey!" she said. "You're Tom Lodge! Great to meet you in person! I'm Mary Quant."

Playing on deck. Caroline South, 1966

We shook hands. I looked around. "It's beautiful. You're a real knock-out.

"Thanks. Here are the new styles to match the music you play," she said proudly.

"I love this gear." I made a quick proposal, "I could speak about them on my show or in my personal appearances?"

"Great," she said without hesitation. "What do you fancy? Help yourself to some."

Less than an hour later I walked out of the boutique wearing a fresh, flamboyant outfit. I hailed a taxi for Caroline House and, with the strut of a peacock, walked into the mansion.

I was greeted by the receptionist. "Wow! You look great, Tom!"

"Thanks, it's from Mary Quant's boutique on the King's Road."

"Ronan wants to see you," she said.

I bounded up the blue carpeted staircase and burst into Ronan's office. I never needed to knock. Ronan was sitting next to Phil Solomon. "Come in, Tom," he said.

"Hi, Ronan."

Ronan looked serious. "You know Phil."

"Sure," I said casually. Phil reached out to shake my hand.

"Phil has been one of our directors for about a year now," Ronan said. "He's been part of what's keeping us afloat. Now he is going to be looking after the programming. He needs to speak with you. I'll leave the two of you together."

I only knew Phil from seeing him around Caroline House. I never had a conversation with him, he always seemed so serious and distant. I knew he owned a music publishing company and a record label but I had no idea that he was one of the directors.

Ronan walked out without saying another word. Phil leaned back in his chair and said, "Yes, we are going to make some changes. We are having some financial difficulties and we have to reorganize."

"What changes?"

"On the programming side, we will be introducing re-cords from my own label, Major Minor Records. Every third record you play will be one of these or some others that I choose. Also, my accountants have made a few suggestions. In order to keep Radio Caroline on-the-air and functioning, we have to cut our expenses and budget."

I felt a pain in my stomach. My heart was beating faster and my hands were becoming sweaty.

"Our operations are going to be tightened. Besides a strict music programming policy, which I will control, we will also have to cut some salaries."

"Mr. Solomon," I said with real urgency, "you are aware that it is our programming that has made us so popular? If you make us play Major Minor's music at regular intervals, we'll lose our audience to Radio London, again. Our pro-gramming is the most unique in all of radio. These deejays are a very special group of people who were chosen per-sonally by me because of their feel for the music scene, the audience and their positive attitudes. We know what works with the music and the listeners. If they have to play your records all the time, they will lose that spark, that quality that has changed this country, the spark that gave us per-mission to be free and explore life with a new British gusto. No, please Mr. Solomon, don't do this!"

"Listen," he said. "I'm not here to negotiate, you can ei-ther take it or leave." He looked away. "And I will be cut-ting your salary in half."

I did not know what to say. A sword had sliced my head in half. All that we had built-up was going to be smashed in one stroke. "I hear you," I said, and walked out the door. I could see that there was no possibility of changing Phil's mind. He was clear, stubborn and adamant. My only course of action, my only chance of a different way, was with Ronan. Also, I was stunned. If I had not walked out at that moment, I would either have lost my temper or burst into tears.

I found Ronan in the record library. "Ronan, what's going on? What's all this slop about Phil Solomon, Major Minor Records and cutting the salaries? I thought we were financially on top. This is the shits. Are you going to let this old fossilized sod destroy Radio Caroline?"

"Calm down, Tom. We overextended ourselves when we took over Caroline South. I'm afraid I can't do anything about it. We have to live with Phil's dictates for awhile, that is, until things get a little better."

I paced the floor. "I don't like it!" I said. "I guess you're giving up?"

"Hey, listen Tom, we don't give up! For you this is just a few months. But we Irish have been fighting this war with the English for over four hundred years. We have never given up. This is not about giving up. This is simply taking a breath and regrouping."

"Well it stinks! And he's cutting my salary in half," I said.

"Yes, I know." Ronan started to say as I paused and took a breath. "But Tom, we are carrying on. It's just a fluke, we've been through worse than this. I know it's hard for you and for everyone else, but I have no choice."

"This is nuts!" I pleaded. "He'll destroy the morale

worse than our Nazi captain or even Wedgwood-Benn. It's like someone blew a fuse on all our positive energy."

"Tom, you are absolutely right. This is difficult but we mustn't lose sight of what we are about. We're in a very special situation. We've cracked a hole in the English establishment's iron control. We've made working-class musicians into multi-millionaires. The kids are having a great time, probably for the first time in their lives. We don't have to put up with England's rigid class system anymore. It's crumbling. No more correct accents or right schooling to get in our way. Tom, a four-hundred-year war between Ireland and England, and by God we're winning, and without violence! We're just playing music and giving our listeners a fun time. That's more powerful than any violence. Do you realize, Tom, the power of music? Music is the sublime currency that is passed between the peoples of the earth. This cannot be destroyed. It's like we're spreading sunshine across this damp, dark land. I still need your help. I need you out there, on-the-air."

Ronan was having an effect on me. I really didn't want to abandon the fight.

He then lowered his voice. "You know there's an old Sufi saying: this too shall pass."

I was deeply touched but I didn't know what to say. I gave Ronan a hug and, with tears in my eyes, I left Caroline House.

I learned later why Ronan's dreams and hopes for Radio Caroline were perhaps a little more intense for him. His grandfather was Michael O'Rahilly, or as he was known, "The O'Rahilly," who took part in the famous Easter uprising of 1916 at the General Post Office in Dublin. During this battle he was killed. The O'Rahilly family also owned the Irish seaport of Greenore, where Ronan outfitted the Radio Caroline ship.

I had been helping Ronan use the blues and rock and roll to not only lighten up straight-laced England, but also to loosen the ties that the English had on the Irish for over four hundred years. This was truly special, but with Phil Solomon at the helm it had gone from being a glorious and unique adventure to a dull profit-making operation.

I drove the hundred miles to my home in the Cotswolds with the top down hoping the wind would blow away my tears, and sat on the hill behind my house to let this all settle. When I came inside Jeanine looked at me, she knew something was wrong.

"I don't know what to do, Phil Solomon has taken over the programming of Radio Caroline and he is killing the spirit."

"You've been through worse than that before," she reassured me. "This is just a bump in the road."

"He cut my salary in half."

Jeanine looked surprised. "Oh, that's no good. Why?"

"To make more money."

"Well mon chéri, so what do you want to do?" she said tenderly.

"I don't know."

We were silent for a while. Finally Jeanine said, "Financially we're all right. The boutique is doing fine and besides, it'll be good to have you here. The boys will really enjoy it."

"Yes, I know," I nodded. But I felt all closed up. What

should I do? Should I leave Caroline? Or should I stick it out and play those dull Major Minor records of Solomon's? I could not see straight. I was angry. The ships were such a phenomenon.

The sad part was that once Phil's programming came into effect, and even though every third record on Radio Caroline was either from Major Minor or one of Phil's choosing, he only had one group that made a showing in the charts and that was the Dubliners with "Seven Drunken Nights." The sound lost its uniqueness.

Then I remembered when I was four years old, my parents and I were on the *Duchess of Richmond*, a passenger ship sailing away from England at the beginning of the war. I had been given a yellow toy car. It was my treasure. I loved it and took it everywhere with me. At meal times it was on my lap and at night it was by my head. Then one day I was playing with it along the rail of the ship. Suddenly the ship's horn blew. I jumped and it fell over the side. I leaned over and watched it hit the water. My heart sank as I watched it sink deeper and deeper into the water. I had the same hollow feeling about Radio Caroline. Something most dear to me was fading away and it looked like it was gone forever.

I tried to cover my sadness by having fun with the boys. They were incredible and so playful. I would romp around on the grass with them, tell them stories. I admired their wonder for life, their non-stop excitement and sense of adventure. But all the time inside I felt colorless and empty.

It slowly became clear to me that it was time to leave Radio Caroline. I was not ready to let my spirit, my love of life and my willingness to risk it all be corralled by Phil Solomon's greed.

Then Jeanine reminded me that I had the ability to make positive changes out of any difficult situation. She would know. She wanted to marry this rich American, Karl Yeager, and though I was over six thousand miles away from her, I refused to be daunted. We laughed as we remembered how I sailed around the world to court her and win her heart.

"You know, Tom," she said, "when you set your mind to it, you can do anything." She gave me a kiss and a hug and added, "And besides, this is your opportunity to do something far more important and maybe even more enjoyable."

"Okay," I said. "Yes, you are right. Thank you."

Suddenly a glow filled my skin, my muscles and my bones. I grabbed Jeanine and we waltzed around and around. I was ready to strike out and embrace new challenges. A week later I phoned Ronan and told him that I had decided not to return to Caroline, that I was ready to explore new avenues. With Phil Solomon's tight bureaucratic programming, the incredible but intangible spirit that had taken us to the top faded into clouds of memory. The deejays played the records and said the words but the magic was gone.

I felt disjointed not being with Radio Caroline. It was as if I had lost a limb. I missed being with my friends, the satisfaction of playing the music and the constant movement of the ship on the rolling seas.

The people still listened but the flame had been blown out. Phil Solomon sold Major Minor records, but now Radio Caroline was just another radio station. This accomplished what the government could not do to that point—kill Caroline. It wasn't long before the disaster was complete. Soon the British government was able to make offshore radio illegal.

I watched and listened from land when on August 14, 1967, the government brought into law the *Marine Broadcasting Offences Act.* One by one the offshore radio stations closed down.

At that time there were ten offshore radio stations around Great Britain. Broadcasting from ocean-anchored ships were Radio Caroline North, Radio Caroline South, Radio London, Britain Radio, Radio England, Radio Scotland and Radio 270. Broadcasting from World War II defense towers out in the ocean were Radio City, Radio Essex and Radio 390. These stations were giving the British people a wide choice of music, from heavy rock to easy listening, from country music to old hits. It was all there.

The new law made it a crime for a British subject to supply the radio stations with water, food, records, fuel or labor. The penalty could be up to two years in jail. Of the ten offshore radio stations that were all around the coast of Great Britain at that time, eight closed down.

Phil Birch, who owned Radio London, said on TV "What the government has done is come up with an imitation of Radio London, which supposedly starts on BBC 1 or Radio One on September 30th. Many of the Radio London deejays have been hired by the BBC to help launch this radio station. They are already copying our jingles, which is very flattering."

But no British law was going to stop Ronan from broadcasting. When interviewed on television he said, "Obviously, with British companies prohibited from advertising, you have to set about it on an international basis, which we have done. Caroline could now be called Caroline International."

For Ronan this was much more than a business. This was an issue of freedom. He outflanked the law by servicing Radio Caroline North from Dublin, Ireland, and Radio Caroline South from Amsterdam, Holland. He employed Irish, Canadian, American or anyone who was not British, but kept a few British rebels, and sold advertising through offices in New York, Paris, Toronto and Tokyo. He was broadcasting into Britain but not touching her shores. No longer did he have Caroline House and he was not using the British ports, so he was again legal.

Since I was British I couldn't work on Caroline, but a number of offers came my way. I did a short stint on BBC Radio One, but found it was too bureaucratic and too controlling. I signed up with an entertainment agent, Bunny Lewis, and was offered the part of the Fool on the Hill for a proposed Beatles film; I believe it was going to be called *The Magical Mystery Tour*. Jeanine's boutique, Sure Shot, was doing well and I was able to spend more time with my three sons. This was a special time with my family, a time to be close and enjoy their young years. This was also a time of rest and making decisions as to what to do next.

It was March 1968 when I phoned Ronan to see how he was doing. He told me our two ships were towed away.

"Who did that?" I asked.

"The Wijsmuller Company, that's the company that looked after our ships."

"Why would they do that?" I asked.

"I heard that the British government made a deal with them."

"What kind of deal?" I asked.

"If we didn't go off-the-air when the government passed the bill making broadcasting from ships illegal, then they wanted our Dutch operating company, the Wijsmuller Company, to have our captains tow us into Amsterdam."

"Why would they want to help the British government?" I asked.

"I was wondering that too, but I heard that in exchange they got that salvage job for the Torrey Canyon. You remember that oil tanker that went aground off Cornwall?"

I was upset. The government had won. It had been a great battle. But nothing could stop the tidal wave of British music that was sweeping the world. It was time for me to move on. How about back to Canada, to the open spaces? Maybe I could once again play the music that stretched the soul? Jeanine was excited to return to Canada and content to close down the boutique. This new adventure was more enticing. Tommy was going to return to the country of his birth, and Brodie and Lionel picked up on our enthusiasm. I would go first and get a deejay job on a radio station and they would follow just as soon as I had found a place to live. I would go to Toronto and stay with my friend, Keith Hampshire, who was already working on a station there. Yes, we needed this and I needed to spread my wings again and play rock and roll.

CHAPTER 16

Professor Lodge

Keith Hampshire, who later recorded the hits "Day-time Night-time," written by Mike Hugg (Manfred Mann's drummer), "The First Cut is the Deepest" and "Big Time Operator," had left Radio Caroline and England in October 1967 and was a deejay in Toronto. When I arrived by ship in Canada in March 1968, he lent me a bed and the use of his car to job hunt. Canada presented new challenges but I was excited. After phoning many radio stations in Ontario I found two openings, one in Smith Falls, near Ottawa, and the other in St. Thomas in southwestern Ontario. I chose CHLO St. Thomas, 68 AM, now 103.9 FM, in nearby London, Ontario.

There was still snow on the ground when I drove west, down the open 401 highway in Keith's blue Volvo. Otis Redding was on the radio singing "(Sitting On) The Dock of the Bay." With the sun shining, it was invigorating to be in this vast country where anything seemed possible. When I arrived at CHLO for my interview with program director Paul Ski, I was met by Dave Longfield, one of the salesmen, who welcomed me and showed me around the station. Even though I still dressed in the wacky clothes of England, had an English accent and was a bit out of place in this conservative environment, I was hired by Paul on the spot and given the evening slot. Maybe he just figured I was a star since he gave a picture taken during my interview with the Beatles much attention.

With my untamed Radio Caroline experiences and now with access to the open transmission of the radio waves, I was free to influence the musical experiences of southwestern Ontario, from teenybopper, bubblegum music to a collage of album, acid and British rock. Led Zeppelin, Jimi Hendrix, Pink Floyd, the Rolling Stones, the Who and such were my normal fare. One record company was not impressed. In fact they were quite upset with me for playing a record I had purchased in Detroit but which had not been released in Canada. This was the first release of Creedence Clearwater Revival's "Suzie Q." My constant playing of this record had the record stores swamped with requests for a disc that was unavailable in Canada. But in the true Radio Caroline spirit, I kept on spinning the record.

For two years I rocked. I did my radio show, introduced bands at the local venues of Don Jones' Wonderland, the Arena, the Western Fair and other clubs in London. I presented the colorful, wild side of Carnaby Street to this part of Canada. The energy of Radio Caroline had arrived on these shores.

From my work on CHLO and doing so many concerts and other community events, I had cemented a close and trusting connection with most of the teens in the area. But I was also creating a reputation among the elders of the community.

My first real connection with the London Arts Community occurred when I received a friendly phone call from a prominent, nationally-renowned local painter, an artist named Greg Curnoe. He thanked me for bringing some inspiring music to the area. Greg introduced me to one of the patrons of the arts, Jay Peterson, who was a director on the Western Fair board. Warm, welcoming and knowledgeable, she was somehow interested in this energetic-music-crazed-Englishman. Jay would invite me into her home on Dufferin Street in London where I met her four teenagers, including Chris, her fourteen-year-old who loved the music I was playing on the radio.

Jay also introduced me to many of the London elders. One of these was Arnold Gingrich, a Mennonite preacher who was working with troubled teens. He asked me if I would help by writing a story based on the four horses of the Apocalypse.

I soon returned with a fairy tale-type story I had written about four horses who lived on the moon. There was the white horse of ideology, the grey horse of poverty, the red horse of war and the black horse of death. Each wanted to rule the earth. One after the other, they came down and spread their nature across the face of the earth. I wrote it as an analogy to current world events. I also made drawings of the horses in their adventures. Arnold was so pleased

1968

with it that he arranged with the Board of Education for me to go around to all the high schools to read the story and show the pictures as slides in their morning assemblies. This led to the Board of Education and the City of London sponsoring me to turn this concept into an arts festival, which we named the Creative Arts Festival. It was held during the spring of 1970 at the Western Fair Grounds. We decided to build the four horses. The high school students who participated were free to express themselves in any art medium. I gave them free rein with no censorship. Their imaginative output was inspiring.

At one of our preparatory meetings for the festival with educational administrators and other people of the arts circle, a tall Englishman with a neat beard approached me. He asked me to come and work for him at Fanshawe College doing whatever I wanted for double the salary I was making as a deejay.

A college! I don't even have a high school diploma. I had left England on my eighteenth birthday to become a cowboy. I had failed all the General Certificate Exams except woodwork. Even though my mother wanted me to keep studying and all my friends were continuing with their education, I was frantic to return to the open spaces. England was suffocating me. I longed for the wild range. And now I was being offered a job to teach or do anything I wanted at a college?

Amazing! "Who are you?" I asked.

"I'm Ricky Atkinson, the Dean of Applied Arts at Fanshawe College."

Being a deejay was a terrific job but this offer was miraculous. I loved the music, of course, but I had learned that at heart I was an adventurer. In fact it was not playing music on the radio that was my passion but the vehicle it provided me. I could explore some of the most creative music, play with sounds, and create a collage of music and words. It was the creative aspect that gave me the most joy.

A short time after the festival I was approached by someone on the City Board and asked if I would supervise a summer drop-in center for the teenagers of the city. I agreed. This was perfect. I quit my job at CHLO, spent the summer running the drop-in center and when September arrived, went to work at Fanshawe College.

To house the drop-in center, the city of London had given us a large, three-story stone building that was an Armory. It was right in the center of London at Richmond Street and Queens Avenue, across from the Millionaires Club. I hired some young teenagers to be my staff, the ones who knew the "scene." I wanted to keep the hard drug pushers out. I also hired artists, yoga teachers and musicians. The program was funded by the money set aside by the Prime Minister Pierre Elliott Trudeau for youth programs. We had rooms for art and exercise, and upstairs there were dormitories.

Outside, some of the teenagers would sit on the steps leading up to our entrance. With their long hair and hippie clothes, they disturbed the millionaires across the street and the respectable bank owners across the other street. But the most troubling thing that we did was to hoist a tie-dye flag from the rooftop flag post. We saw it as an expression of art but the veterans saw it as an insult to the Canadian nationalism and the Maple Leaf flag. Once the summer was over and we all headed away, the city demolished the building, erasing our existence.

I headed to Fanshawe College and, for the first few weeks, I wandered around the campus wondering what to do.

The college on the west side of the city consisted of four large sprawling buildings with grass lawns and trees. Originally it had been a technical college but in 1967 the Ontario government converted it into a community college. I was in D Block, which housed a large Applied Arts campus for painting, silkscreen, sculpture, television, radio and journalism. It was a modern, spacious building around which I walked, doing nothing or whatever I liked. I explored and spoke with the faculty and students, and soon an idea began to emerge. It was an idea of how to use the materials of this college, these students and my endless time. This was an idea that came from the very foundation of my way of life.

Prior to this, while at CHLO, I had also begun working with Marshall McLuhan and Buckminster Fuller at seminars they held. While I was still with CHLO, I would attend McLuhan's workshops at the University of Toronto. Their approaches to life resonated deeply with my own inner feelings about the world and life. McLuhan had coined the word "media" just a few years earlier, and that was the field I wanted to explore. Also, one summer I took the family down to Carbondale, Illinois, to the University of Southern

Illinois, so that I could work with Buckminster Fuller. My enthusiasm for the work of these two was extreme, so it was natural that my first idea to share with interested students at the college was their work.

I started to create an extracurricular course in the college that was available to every student at the time but I soon realized that to really make this work, I needed to have full-time students. I needed to bring this up with Ricky.

Ricky Atkinson's office was beyond a large secretary office, which was broken up with movable partitions. I had an office that was partitioned in the corner that was only a few feet away from Ricky's door.

One morning I knocked on his door. "Ricky," I said. "This idea of my course is becoming so popular with the students that we need to create a full-time program. It cannot work just with these extracurricular students."

He was sitting at his desk with a large window behind that looked out onto a field. On his office walls were some of his paintings. "What would the course cover?" he asked.

"It would be a practical exploration of the theoretical work of McLuhan and Fuller," I said. "We would explore everything that was involved with electricity, like radio, television, film, laser beams, electronic music, electric guitars and biofeedback. We'll examine everything in the electronic environment. In the same way a painter explores expression through color and form or a sculptor explores materials and shape, we would explore the art form of electronics."

"Interesting," he mused. "This would be a creative arts course?" he asked.

"Yes. It would be a course of the creative aspects of electronics. It would be open-ended. It would cover all that is happening in electronics today. All media would be material for our work."

Ricky got up from his desk, came around and sat in a chair near me. "What would you call this course?" he asked.

"Well, let's see," I said. "It is a creative course about electronics. How about we call it Creative Electronics?"

"Do you already have some interested students who would leave an existing course and join yours?"

"Oh yes and also some of the students who worked with me at the Creative Arts Festival and the drop-in center. There will be no problem in getting full-time students," I said.

Ricky went back to his desk and made some notes, "Okay, so here's what we'll do," he said. "You can have twelve students. That's the limit for now. I'll give you a classroom and a budget to purchase the equipment. But first bring me the names of the students who want to join you."

I left elated. I knew instantly who my choices for the twelve students would be. When I told them, they were delighted to be chosen as full-time students in Creative Electronics. This was a student's dream. There was no curriculum. There was no preliminary. It was open-ended, a program of exploration and discovery.

We started with a bang, covering the strange sounds of electronic music and laser beams. Now we needed a recording studio. Soon Ricky gave us another classroom in A Block into which we built our small recording studio. It had a small recording booth with basic equipment but enough to capture what we needed. The first band that recorded there was with Chris Peterson and Jamie James—later James toured with Steppenwolf and then formed the Kingbees, which was quite a popular local-band in Hollywood. Rock and roll had arrived at Fanshawe College.

I was able to accomplish all this because I didn't have enough experience or knowledge to know it couldn't be done. I did not have any academic background nor was I immersed in bureaucratic practice. What I did have was a street sense. In fact some in the college felt I was a little too much at times, but this was the beauty of my working with Ricky. He understood the ways of bureaucracy and at the same time enjoyed the energy of the creative spirit. He was the perfect buffer between me and the rest of the college.

In going into the second year, the enthusiasm for the course was so strong that we were given another large space to build a second recording studio (D 1048) and a good-sized budget to buy all the necessary equipment.

There was one problem. We had no idea how to build a professional recording studio. This became our school project and field trip. We went off to Toronto to pick the brains of the experts. We visited Toronto Sound Studio, Jack Richardson's Nimbus Nine Studio and recording studio suppliers such as Studer. We also took a field trip down to New York state to visit the electronic music genius Robert Moog.

Building this studio was a major undertaking. We had to cut a space in the foundation to create isolation between the studio and the control room. We built concrete block walls on each side of the cut and filled the blocks with sand to help dampen the transmission of sound. We used all the advice we had received from the experts to kill the room's natural resonance. This gave us full control of the sounds being recorded. As we did this work, the students were learning everything from acoustics to the electronic layout of a recording studio.

Then suddenly in 1973, OPEC imposed an oil embargo and it seemed like the price doubled overnight. The whole Western world went into shock. All our freewheeling lifestyle, our easy success suddenly came to a screaming halt. Ricky called me into his office.

"This OPEC business is creating a big problem for us," he said. Ricky looked more serious than I had ever seen him. He always had a positive air about him. Even when I used to barge into his office with my requests for more funds, more college space and more openness with college policies, he always welcomed me and treated me with intelligence and understanding.

At times my insistence, my pushiness in expanding the program must have been a concern with his need to keep the whole ship of Applied Arts on an even keel. He had always been most accommodating with me. But today he looked disturbed. "We are going to have to drastically cut budgets," he continued. I remained silent, waiting for the bad news. "The Board of Governors has said that we may have to cut all the programs in the college that are not career-oriented, and that could include Creative Electronics."

"Career-oriented? That's interesting. If I can make Creative Electronics career-oriented then we'll survive, right?" I asked.

"Yes, of course. But how can you? That is always the difficulty with arts programs. The bureaucrats very rarely see the importance of art because there's no immediate benefit."

"Just give me one week," I said as I rushed out of his office and went straight to my phone. I called up all my contacts in Toronto and asked them all one question. "What, today, does the Canadian music industry lack?" And everyone had the same answer: "Good, professional record producers and, knowledgeable and efficient recording engineers."

They explained that in 1971 the Canadian Radio and Television Commission had mandated that radio stations must play thirty percent Canadian content in their music programming. The radio stations were disappointed with the poor quality in the record productions. Even though Canada was developing some fine artists, the homegrown productions were an embarrassment for the stations.

That was it! I would transform Creative Electronics into a training ground for record producers and recording engineers. We already had the studio.

What I now needed was a new name and an advisory board for this new program. For the advisory board I recruited my contacts at the recording studios as well as John Mills from the Performing Right Society of CAPAC and the President of Capitol Records of Canada.

The name "Creative Electronics" would not be acceptable as a name for a professional training ground for record producers and recording engineers. This program was for the music industry but it also was in the Applied Arts division of the college. So the name was obvious. I named the program Music Industry Arts (MIA). It would contain two separate career streams, one for record producers and one for recording engineers. Our standards were set by the needs of the Canadian music industry.

The day these esteemed representatives of the Canadian music industry arrived at the college for our first advisory board meeting, they caused quite a stir. "Some of them look a little Mafioso," Ricky said with a great big smile and a laugh.

We were still taking over more and more space in the college, creating the world's first training program for record producers and recording engineers. As a result, we received over a thousand applications for seventy-five places. The criteria for being in Music Industry Arts were that the student had to be a musician, preferably one that has been on the road, but at least one that had played in local bars. The student also had to pass an audition. I wanted musicians who were recording in the studio to relate to musicians on the other side of the glass, people who thought and spoke the same language they did. In the past, many of the engineers had been technicians and many of the producers had been salesmen. We were going to change that.

I soon gathered around me a staff of impressive professionals. There was music arranger Jan Wetstein (now Jan Greene who, after I left, became the MIA Coordinator, running and improving the program for more than twenty years); record producer and singer/composer Terry McManus; Eric McLuhan (Marshall McLuhan's son); sculptor Michael Hayden; recording engineer Bill Seddon; recording engineer Paul Steenhuis and many other outstanding experts.

Then in 1978 I was also invited to join a few others in

setting up a college radio station 6X FM, 106.9. I felt it had the same cutting-edge spirit as Radio Caroline.

This is how MIA became the foundation for a new emerging Canadian music industry. It started as a bohemian/hippie experimental course and then had grown into the creator of many of Canada's top career positions with its graduates becoming executives in record companies, music publishing companies and recording studios. At last all seemed peaceful. I had a satisfying regular job, and my family and I were settled in a comfortable house. Best of all I was still involved in the music that I loved.

CHAPTER 17

An Idea That
Can't Be Silenced

I am constantly reminded of the effect that Radio Caroline had on the youth of Britain and of the influence we had on music and culture across the United Kingdom and then around the world.

I hear from old friends. I get letters from people who remember how it was for them. I receive inquiries from newspapers and magazines, websites and radio stations that are discovering the magic and spirit of Radio Caroline for the first time.

I often think about our listeners, the unseen public, separated from us by miles of water. Each day I would speak to them from out at sea and play my favorite music.

Not too long ago, I received a letter from a listener back in those days. Alan Milewczyk wrote: "Tom, you will never know just how much you did for me, a young shy kid, grow-

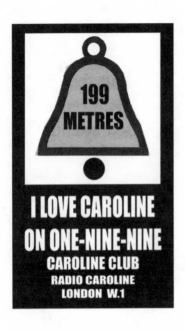

ing up in the slums of Manchester. It was on Easter Sunday 1964 that I first heard of Radio Caroline. There was an article on the front page of the *Sunday Times*, no less, saying that a new music station was about to commence broadcasting, anchored off the Essex coast. I was 14, at a boys only grammar school in Manchester, and heavily into pop music but very unsatisfied by the restricted output from the BBC Light Programme. There were only a few programs a week when you could hear the latest records—*Saturday Club*, *Easy Beat* and, of course, *Pick of the Pops*—but they just weren't enough. We had Radio Luxembourg at night but the signal was prone to fading and, in any case, they didn't play records the whole way through on their programs, which were sponsored by the record companies."

He was able to listen a little on the family radio but the signal was weak. Then Radio Caroline sailed north to the Isle of Man. "I was absolutely delighted. Even though we would be about 100 miles from the ship, most of the distance was over the Irish Sea, so I had a fair idea we would have pretty good reception in Manchester.

"Caroline was the talk of the class—my schoolmates who had heard the news, were quizzing me where to find Caroline on the dial. I was in demand.

"Our Philips radio had one of those tuning 'magic eyes,' it was completely full, the signal was as strong as it could get. The music was just beaming in loud and clear. I heard all the hits of the day: 'The House of the Rising Sun,' 'It's All Over Now,' 'Hold Me,' 'It's Over' and 'Nobody I Know.'

"I loved the music that they were playing, not just the UK hits, but also records from the American Hot 100. It was the first time I really heard R&B.

"My classmates all felt the same way; Caroline spoke for our generation. For the first time, we had something that was ours. It was such an exciting time and we all felt a part of the major social changes that were sweeping the nation. At the heart of it all was Caroline on One-Nine-Nine."

This, then, is what Radio Caroline meant to the youth of the United Kingdom. Most of them were born in the immediate aftermath of World War II and were hungry for a life different from their parents. Music was the first step toward independence. All of us together were right there at the beginning of a transformation.

And the driving force behind it all, the strength of Radio Caroline was, of course, Ronan O'Rahilly. It was his energy and relentless determination that bound us together and kept us together.

THE RISE AND FALL OF CAROLINE TELEVISION

I had been at Fanshawe College for a while. Music Industry Arts (MIA) was swamped with applications from all over the country, from people who wanted to be recording engineers or record producers. The program's demand had

Ronan gives a thumb-up to Radio Caroline South, 1965

outstripped all my expectations. MIA was becoming known throughout Canada and the United States.

One day I received a call from Ronan.

"I have a new project going," he said.

"Are you going to put the ship back on-the-air?"

"That may happen. But I'm working on a television idea. Caroline Television."

"What?" I said with astonishment. "Caroline Television?"

"Yes! It's happening, baby! We're outfitting two DC-3 airplanes in Spain."

"Airplanes? That's something else!"

"Fun, eh!" he laughed. "They will take turns flying in circles over the North Sea as they broadcast. Their signal will cover the entire UK."

"You're amazing!"

Ronan often seemed to me to be one step ahead of the unusual. He had that way of suggesting the impossible, and then with a heavy dose of Irish charm, making you believe that it was possible. He would persuade you with such conviction that you would in turn try to make it happen. Now he wanted to have two DC-3 planes circling over the North Sea broadcasting television. I was speechless but intrigued.

"You want to join us?"

"I don't think so, Ronan. I've got a great thing going on here in Canada. We're creating a Canadian music industry."

"Pity. Otherwise we'd put you on television."

"How are you going to broadcast from an airplane?"

"You'll have a camera on you," Ronan explained. "You'll be operating the camera while broadcasting little films recorded on video tape."

I understood the concept. For some time, bands had been making films of their music. In fact, after Kit Lambert, the manager of the Who, had rented an office at Caroline House, the band used the building's grand staircases and rooms to make a short film directed by Michael Lindsey Hogg for their hit, "Happy Jack."

In 1967 Ampex had introduced the VR-3000 portable broadcast video recorder. For the first time, recorded television was more widely available.

This was such a novel idea. Being on a ship broadcasting from the ocean was one thing, but being on a plane and operating a reel to reel video tape recorder seemed unusually challenging.

"Ronan, you never stop. That's an unbelievable idea!"

Ronan laughed. "And here's the clincher, Tommy. I've

already asked John Lennon, Marshall McLuhan and a few other artists to make short video tape recordings of their work. And they've all agreed. It's really happening."

"Music television? What a novel concept!!"

"The advertisers are already lining up for business," Ronan said. "They know of our previous good work. I have been in touch with J. Walter Thompson [the advertising agency] and they're all for it. They said the airplanes are like having a very tall mast."

I was becoming enthusiastic. "When do you go on-the-air?"

Ronan sounded hesitant. "As soon as we sort out a technical problem. We are having difficulty keeping the signal steady while we're in flight. Can you help us with that?"

I thought for a moment. This was a great coincidence. I had just been talking with a technician back in the States. "Yes, I believe I can solve that problem," I told him. "Just give me a couple of days."

"I'll have Jim, my technician, call you. Okay, Tom baby, you're a good friend. Cheers, for now."

I had been in touch with some broadcast technicians from Purdue University in Lafayette, Indiana for one of the projects I was doing with my students. The university had developed a way of broadcasting educational television programs into the Appalachians from an airplane. I called them up and asked if they could send me the technical blueprints. "No problem," they said. The blueprints arrived in a week and I shipped them straight off to Ronan.

A few weeks later, I phoned Ronan to see how Caroline Television was coming along. "Not so good," he said.

"Didn't the blueprints fix the problem?"

"Oh yes, they were just fine. But just before we were ready to go on-the-air, someone blew up both our planes."

"Who would do that?" I asked.

Ronan had developed a deep suspicion of governments. He had better reasons than most.

"Who knows for sure," he said. "Maybe it was MI5 or the SAS. But anyway, it had to be some government thing. But not to worry, I've bought back the MV *Mi Amigo*. Radio Caroline is going back on-the-air."

Ronan never quit. He could not create Caroline Television, so he was going to re-launch Radio Caroline in the North Sea. I hung up the phone and walked around the college feeling a wonder for Ronan and how he had inspired me. With his non-stop flow of ideas, he is the most stimulating person I've ever met.

I realized at that moment how Ronan had taught me that the only ceiling to your life is your own mind. I was creating something remarkable with MIA. There were students committed to their music. There were students in the two recording studios delving deep into the innovations of multi-track recording. There was an excitement from students being in a place where the encouragement for their creativity seemed endless.

Even though Caroline Television didn't work out, my amazement at Ronan's creativity has only grown. He took note of an emerging technology and conceived of a music television channel eleven years before MTV came along. Then he got others, like Lennon and McLuhan, interested as well.

RADIO CAROLINE LIVES

Ronan O'Rahilly gave to all of us that worked on Radio Caroline one of the finest opportunities possible for expressing ourselves and our views about life. Ronan's tireless pursuit of freedom of expression for all who desire it offers lessons for all of us. Radio Caroline showed that no obstacle is too high to surmount—even if it is a powerful government.

With Radio Caroline, Ronan kept his dream—and ours—alive. Once the British Establishment licensed commercial radio on land, they still had created a broadcasting system that was tightly controlled. BBC Radio One was launched as a pop music station on the September 30, 1967, to compensate for the loss of the offshore radio stations. Commercial radio entered on land with Capital Radio, on October 6, 1973, licensed and controlled by the government.

Resisting this authority, Ronan re-purchased the MV *Mi Amigo* and once again defied the government from the iso-

Aboard Radio Caroline, 1995

lation and freedom of the North Sea. That was until March 19, 1980, when storms sank and finished off the *Mi Amigo*. But nothing was going to stop Ronan. Soon he purchased another rebel ship, the *Ross Revenge*, a deep-sea trawler, and on August 19, 1983, Radio Caroline went back on-the-air for another six years.

On August 19, 1989, the Dutch vessel *Volans* approached the *Ross Revenge*, and while the British launch HMS *Land-ward* was standing by, armed men from the *Volans* boarded Radio Caroline. The crew of the *Ross Revenge* tried to resist the invasion but the Dutch crew used force and gained control of the ship. Throughout this ordeal, the conflict was being broadcast play-by-play from our transmitters to an astonished audience. But even once the transmitter was silenced and the ship was stripped of broadcast equipment, the crew refused to leave the vessel. They waited until the

Tom Lodge, 2009

raiders had left and then somehow managed to go back on the air. That was until the government and further storms silenced her on November 5, 1990.

But still, Radio Caroline was not to be silenced. In the nineties, as the government became a little more amiable, Ronan received a few one-month special licenses to broadcast from the *Ross Revenge*, but always with tight government control and only an extremely weak broadcast signal. Even so, I was delighted.

I went back and did a few broadcasts in England while she was at sea off Clacton-on-Sea. Our legal signal was too weak to reach London but still we loved the nostalgia. It was such a joy to be out at sea again, broadcasting music, feeling the rolling of the ship's floor and the familiar ocean smells. Even though we were no longer quite the "pirates" we once were, we were still at sea, playing the music we loved. Later,

I went with the ship and broadcast from the London Docks, and then at Southend-On-Sea.

May 1, 2001 saw Radio Caroline broadcasting from Astra 1G satellite and on weekend evenings on the Rock of the Riviera, 88.4 FM to the French and Italian Rivieras. It wasn't long before she was broadcasting all over the UK from Sky satellite.

In 2004 she entered the Internet and this, yet again, rekindled the broadcast fire in me. I joined Radio Caroline with my son Tom Lodge Junior doing a weekly show until April 2007, when I proudly handed the reins over to my son.

What Ronan began is still with us today. Caroline is now run by Peter Moore, with Ronan in the background—who still serves as our mentor and inspiration.

Sure, the battle to have the kind of music we want, and play and listen to it when we want, is much easier now than in those days. We, all of us, won that right. But Radio Caroline also exists today as a reminder of how important freedom of expression is in every society. And whenever governments and those in control try to restrict and crush our creative spirit, we all suffer.

There is always an established social structure that is continually endeavoring to seal, reinforce and maintain its control over society. In good times, however, we have a tendency to grow complacent. When we do, those in power try to assert themselves and further dominate our lives.

This controlling force needs to have its systems periodically opened up to the unpredictable and to the fresh air. Radio Caroline not only stands for this opening, but also for new birth, for creativity, and above all, for the joy of freedom. As Leonard Cohen once wrote, "There's a crack in everything, and that's how the light gets in."

Onboard the ship, we had the isolation and the rolling seas to encourage our non-conformity. But even on land we can let the example of Radio Caroline, and the echoes we hear from the music she plays, illustrate the joy of being adventurous and following our passions.

I am here, always ready to do my part. Send the tender to pick me up.

Radio Caroline Hits

These are some of the groups and artists, and their releases, that Radio Caroline made into hits. Although there were other radio stations at the time, Radio Caroline, with two ships broadcasting, was covering the whole of the UK and was the dominant influence. Also Radio Caroline influenced the music creators to be daring and this, in turn, influenced the audience to appreciate new sounds.

The following is the date and the position in the charts that these releases reached in the UK and USA. In the UK the positions are recorded by *Record World/Music Week* and in the USA are recorded by *Billboard*.

Artist	Single Release	Date m/y	Top Pos in UK	Top Pos in US
Alan Price Set	I Put a Spell on You	4/66	14	xx
	Hi-Lili, Hi-Lo	8/66	12	xx
	Simon Smith & His Amazing Dancing Bear	4/67	5	xx
	The House That Jack Built	9/67	11	xx
	Don't Stop the Carnival	2/68	18	xx
Amen Corner	Gin House Blues	8/67	17	xx
	Bend Me, Shape Me	2/68	4	xx
Animals	House of the Rising Sun	7/64	1	1
	I'm Crying	10/64	10	xx
	Don't Let Me Be Misunderstood	2/65	9	xx
	Bring it On Home to Me	5/65	7	xx
	We Gotta Get out of This Place	8/65	2	xx
	It's My Life	11/65	7	xx
	Inside-Looking Out	3/66	15	xx
	Don't Bring Me Down	6/66	7	12
	San Francisco Nights	11/67	8	xx
Beach Boys	I Get Around	8/64	8	1
	Barbara Ann	3/66	3	2
	Sloop John B	5/66	2	3
	God Only Knows	9/66	3	39
	Good Vibrations	12/66	3	1
	Then I Kissed Hr	5/67	13	xx
	Heroes and Villains	9/67	10	xx
	Darlin'	2/68	13	xx
Beatles	Can't Buy Me Love	4/64	1	1

Artist	Single Release	Date m/y	Top Pos in UK	Top Pos in US
Beatles (*cont'd*)	Hard Days Night	8/64	1	1
	I Feel Fine	12/64	1	1
	Ticket to Ride	5/65	1	1
	Help!	8/65	1	1
	Day Tripper/We Can Work it Out	1/66	1	1
	Paperback Writer	7/66	7	1
	Yellow Submarine/ Eleanor Rigby	9/66	2	2
	Penny Lane/ Strawberry Fields	3/67	2	1
	All You Need is Love	8/67	2	1
	Hello Goodbye	12/67	1	1
	Magical Mystery Tour (EP)	1/68	2	1
Jeff Beck	Hi Ho Silver Lining	5/67	15	xx
Bee Gees	New York Mining Disaster 1941	5/67	19	14
	Massachusetts	10/67	1	11
	World	12/67	10	xx
	Words	2/68	15	15
Len Barry	1-2-3	12/65	4	2
	Like a Baby	2/66	12	27
Chuck Berry	No Particular Place to Go	6/64	4	10
Cilla Black	You're My World	6/64	1	26
	It's For You	9/64	14	79
	Alfie	4/66	15	95
	Don't Answer Me	7/66	12	xx
	A Fool Am I	11/66	16	xx
Box Tops	The Letter	10/67	5	1

Artist	Single Release	Date m/y	Top Pos in UK	Top Pos in US
Byrds	Mr. Tambourine Man	7/65	4	5
Cream	I Feel Free	1/67	17	xx
Dave Clark Five	Can't You See That She's Mine	6/64	12	4
	Catch Us If You Can	8/65	5	4
	Everybody Knows	12/67	6	43
John Fred & His Playboy Band	Judy in Disguise (With Glasses)	2/68	5	1
Dave Davies	Death of a Clown	8/67	4	xx
Dave Dee, Dozy, Beaky, Mick & Tich	Hold Tight!	4/66	2	xx
	Hide Away	7/66	10	xx
	Bend It!	10/66	2	xx
	Save Me	1/67	7	xx
	Touch Me, Touch Me	4/67	20	xx
	Okay!	6/67	11	xx
	Zabadak!	11/67	3	52
	Legend of Xanadu	3/68	2	xx
Bob Dylan	Times They Are a-Changin'	4/65	7	xx
	Subterranean Homesick Blues	5/65	12	39
	Like a Rolling Stone	9/65	5	2
	Positively 4th Street	11/65	13	7
	Rainy Day Women #12 & 35	6/66	11	2
	I Want You	8/66	19	20

Artist	Single Release	Date m/y	Top Pos in UK	Top Pos in US
Donovan	Catch the Wind	4/65	4	23
	Sunshine Superman	1/67	4	1
	Mellow Yellow	3/67	11	2
	There is a Mountain	11/67	10	11
	Jennifer Juniper	3/68	5	6
Easybeats	Friday on My Mind	12/66	5	16
Marianne Faithfull	As Tears Go By	9/64	9	22
Georgie Fame	Yeh Yeh	1/65	1	21
	Get Away	7/66	4	xx
	Sunny	10/66	15	xx
	Sitting in the Park	1/67	13	xx
	Ballad of Bonnie Clyde	1/68	3	7
Flower Pot Men	Let's Go to San Francisco	9/67	7	xx
Wayne Fontana	Um Um Um Um Um Um	11/64	7	xx
	Game of Love	2/65	8	1
Four Tops	Reach Out I'll Be There	11/66	1	1
	Standing in the Shadows of Love	2/67	15	6
	Bernadette	4/67	14	4
	Seven Rooms of Gloom	7/67	17	14
	Walk Away Renée	1/68	4	14
Fortunes	You've Got Your Troubles	8/65	3	7
	This Golden Ring	3/66	20	82
Foundations	Baby, Now That I've Found You	11/67	1	11

Artist	Single Release	Date m/y	Top Pos in UK	Top Pos in US
Four Seasons	Rag Doll	10/64	5	1
	Let's Hang On!	1/66	7	11
	I've Got You Under My Skin	11/66	19	9
Aretha Franklin	Respect	7/67	13	1
Jimi Hendrix	Hey Joe	2/67	10	xx
	Purple Haze	5/67	8	65
	The Wind Cries Mary	6/67	10	xx
Herd	From the Underworld	11/67	7	xx
Herman's Hermits	I'm into Something Good	10/64	3	13
	Silhouettes	3/65	3	5
	Oh No Not My Baby	5/65	11	xx
	Just a Little Bit Better	9/65	20	7
	No Milk Today	11/66	10	35
	There's a Kind of Hush	3/67	7	4
	I Can Take or Leave Your Loving	2/68	12	22
Hollies	Just One Look	4/64	6	44
	Here I Go Again	6/64	5	xx
	We're Through	10/64	11	xx
	Yes I Will	3/65	10	xx
	I'm Alive	7/65	1	xx
	Look Through Any Window	10/65	7	32
	I Can't Let Go	3/66	6	42
	Bus Stop	7/66	6	5
	Stop! Stop! Stop!	11/66	2	7
	On a Carousel	3/67	6	11
	Carrie Anne	6/67	9	9

Artist	Single Release	Date m/y	Top Pos in UK	Top Pos in US
Honeycombs	Have I the Right?	9/64	1	5
	That's the Way	9/65	13	xx
Paul Jones	High Time	11/66	4	xx
	I've Been A Bad, Bad Boy	2/67	3	xx
Tom Jones	It's Not Unusual	3/65	1	10
	What's New Pussycat?	9/65	14	3
	Green Green Grass of Home	12/66	1	11
	Detroit City	3/67	9	27
	Funny Familiar Forgotten Feeling	5/67	7	49
	I'll Never Fall in Love Again	9/67	2	6
	I'm Coming Home	12/67	5	57
	Delilah	3/68	6	15
Kinks	You Really Got Me	9/64	2	7
	All Day and All of the Night	11/64	5	7
	Tired of Waiting for You	2/65	2	6
	Everybody's Gonna Be Happy	4/65	18	xx
	Set Me Free	6/65	14	23
	See My Friend	9/65	18	xx
	Till the End of the Day	1/66	8	50
	Dedicated Follower of Fashion	4/66	9	36
	Sunny Afternoon	7/66	1	14
	Dead End Street	12/66	7	73
	Waterloo Sunset	6/67	3	xx
	Autumn Almanac	11/67	4	xx
Bob Lind	Elusive Butterfly	3/66	19	5

Artist	Single Release	Date m/y	Top Pos in UK	Top Pos in US
Long John Baldry	Let the Heartaches Begin	12/67	3	88
Los Bravos	Black is Black	8/66	2	4
Lovin' Spoonful	Daydream	5/66	3	2
	Summer in the City	8/66	9	1
Lulu	Shout	6/64	10	94
Mamas & the Papas	Monday Monday	6/66	2	1
	Dedicated to the One I Love	5/67	2	2
	Creeque Alley	8/67	12	5
Manfred Mann	Hubble Bubble Toil and Trouble	5/64	20	xx
	Do Wah Diddy Diddy	8/64	2	1
	Sha La La	11/64	3	12
	Come Tomorrow	2/65	5	50
	If You Gotta Go, Go Now	10/65	2	xx
	Pretty Flamingo	5/66	1	29
	Just Like a Woman	9/66	11	xx
	Semi-Detached Suburban Mr. James	11/66	3	xx
	Ha Ha Said the Clown	4/67	8	xx
	Mighty Quinn	2/68	2	10
McCoys	Hang On Sloopy	10/65	6	1
Barry McGuire	The Eve of Destruction	10/65	3	1
Scott McKenzie	San Francisco (Be Sure to Wear Flowers in Your Hair)	8/67	1	14

Artist	Single Release	Date m/y	Top Pos in UK	Top Pos in US
Millie	My Boy Lollipop	5/64	2	2
Mindbenders	A Groovy Kind of Love	3/66	1	2
Moody Blues	Go Now	1/65	5	10
Move	Night of Fear	2/67	6	xx
	I Can Hear the Grass Grow	4/67	19	xx
	Flowers in the Rain	10/67	4	xx
	Fire Brigade	3/68	3	xx
Nashville Teens	Tobacco Road	8/64	6	14
	Google Eye	11/64	13	xx
Roy Orbison	It's Over	6/64	2	9
	Oh, Pretty Woman	10/64	1	1
	Pretty Paper	12/64	6	15
	Lana	7/66	19	xx
	Too Soon to Know	9/66	4	68
Wilson Pickett	In the Midnight Hour	10/65	17	21
Pink Floyd	See Emily Play	7/67	8	xx
Pretty Things	Don't Bring Me Down	11/64	14	xx
	Honey I Need	3/65	19	xx
Procol Harum	A Whiter Shade of Pale	6/67	1	5
	Homburg	10/67	9	34
Otis Redding	My Girl	2/66	16	xx
	(Sitting On) The Dock of the Bay	3/68	8	1

Artist	Single Release	Date m/y	Top Pos in UK	Top Pos in US
Righteous Brothers	You've Lost That Lovin' Feelin'	2/65	1	1
Rolling Stones	It's All Over Now	7/64	4	26
	Little Red Rooster	12/64	4	xx
	The Last Time	3/65	5	9
	(I Can't Get No) Satisfaction	9/65	1	1
	Get Off of My Cloud	11/65	1	1
	19th Nervous Breakdown	2/66	8	2
	Paint It, Black	6/66	4	1
	Have You Seen Your Mother, Baby...	10/66	6	9
	Let's Spend the Night Together/Ruby Tuesday	2/67	2	1
	We Love You/Dandelion	9/67	8	14
Sam The Sham & the Pharaohs	Wooly Bully	7/65	17	2
Searchers	Don't Throw Your Love Away	5/64	1	16
Seekers	I'll Never Find Another You	3/65	2	4
	A World of Our Own	5/65	4	xx
	The Carnival is Over	12/65	1	xx
	Someday One Day	4/66	17	xx
	Walk With Me	10/66	11	68
	Morningtown Ride	1/67	2	44
	Georgy Girl	3/67	8	2
	Where Will the Good Apples Fall	10/67	12	xx

Artist	Single Release	Date m/y	Top Pos in UK	Top Pos in US
Simon & Garfunkel	Homeward Bound	5/66	12	5
Percy Sledge	When a Man Loves a Woman	6/66	5	1
Small Faces	Whatcha Gonna Do About It	10/65	18	xx
	Sha La La La Lee	3/66	2	xx
	Hey Girl	6/66	13	xx
	All or Nothing	9/66	1	xx
	My Mind's Eye	12/66	6	xx
	Here Comes the Nice	7/67	15	xx
	Itchycoo Park	9/67	5	16
	Tin Soldier	1/68	14	73
Spencer Davis Group	Keep On Running	1/66	2	76
	Somebody Help Me	4/66	1	47
	When I Come Home	9/66	20	xx
	Gimme Some Loving	11/66	8	7
	I'm a Man	2/67	16	10
Dusty Springfield	I Just Don't Know What to Do with Myself	8/64	7	xx
	Losing You	12/64	13	91
	Some of Your Lovin'	10/65	13	xx
	You Don't Have to Say You Love Me	5/66	4	4
	Going Back	7/66	18	xx
	All I See Is You	10/66	9	20
Sonny & Cher	I Got You Babe	9/65	3	1
	Baby Don't Go	10/65	11	8
	What Now My Love	3/66	18	14

Artist	Single Release	Date m/y	Top Pos in UK	Top Pos in US
Sonny & Cher				
(cont'd)	Little Man	10/66	8	21
Status Quo	Pictures of			
	Matchstick Men	2/68	10	12
Supremes	Where Did Our Love Go	10/64	2	1
	Baby Love	11/64	1	1
	Stop! In the			
	Name of Love	4/65	9	1
	You Can't Hurry Love	10/66	5	1
	You Keep Me Hangin' On	12/66	14	1
	The Happening	6/67	5	1
	Reflections	10/67	7	2
Them	Baby, Please Don't Go	2/65	13	xx
	Here Comes the Night	4/65	6	24
Traffic	Paper Sun	6/67	15	94
	Hole in My Shoe	10/67	3	xx
	Here We Go Round			
	the Mulberry Bush	12/67	14	xx
Tremeloes	Here Comes My Baby	3/67	5	13
	Silence is Golden	6/67	2	11
	Even the Bad			
	Times Are Good	9/67	6	36
	Suddenly You Love Me	2/68	7	44
Troggs	Wild Thing	5/66	7	1
	With a Girl Like You	8/66	1	29
	I Can't Control Myself	11/66	6	43
	Any Way That			
	You Want Me	1/67	9	xx
	Give it to Me	3/67	15	xx
	Love is All Around	11/67	6	7

Artist	Single Release	Date m/y	Top Pos in UK	Top Pos in US
Turtles	Happy Together	3/67	18	6
	She'd Rather Be With Me	6/67	4	4
Ike & Tina Turner	River Deep, Mountain High	7/66	2	88
Unit 4 + 2	Concrete and Clay	4/65	3	28
Dionne Warwick	Walk on By	5/64	10	6
Who	I Can't Explain	4/65	8	93
	Anyway, Anyhow, Anywhere	7/65	12	xx
	My Generation	12/65	3	74
	Substitute	4/66	6	xx
	I'm a Boy	10/66	3	xx
	Happy Jack	1/67	3	24
	Pictures of Lily	5/67	6	51
	I Can See for Miles	11/67	15	9
Stevie Wonder	I Was Made to Love Her	8/67	5	2
Yardbirds	For Your Love	4/65	2	6
	Heart Full of Soul	7/65	2	9
	Evil Hearted You/Still I'm Sad	10/65	14	xx
	Shapes of Things	3/66	12	11
	Over Under Sideways Down	6/66	12	13
Young Rascals	Groovin'	6/67	18	1
Zombies	She's Not There	9/64	13	2
	Tell Her No	2/65	xx	12

About the Author

TOM LODGE

Tom Lodge was born in 1936 in a cottage in the Surrey village of Forest Green, England.

His grandfather was Sir Oliver Lodge, a scientist and the inventor of wireless technology in 1894, two years before Marconi. A plaque was installed by the Royal Society in 1995 at Oxford University Museum of Natural History to commemorate this event. Many other innovations and inventions are credited to him, including the spark plug and the loudspeaker.

Tom's father, Oliver W.F. Lodge was a poet, painter and a professor at William and Mary in Virginia, and other schools and was part of the so-called, "Bloomsbury set," the group of writers, artists and intellectuals that included Virginia Woolf, John Maynard Keynes, E. M. Forster, Lytton Strachey, Duncan Grant and Vanessa Bell. Tom's mother Diana, a painter, was also a member.

When World War II broke out the Lodge family was evacuated from England and Tom spent part of his youth in Gloucester County, Virginia .

At the end of the war they returned to England and lived near Painswick, Gloucestershire. Tom was educated at Bedales School, a boarding school, where he developed an interest in music. He took lessons on the violin and the clarinet and also taught himself the guitar and harmonica. He played the stand up Bass in a four piece skiffle band, called the "Top Flat Ramblers." At seventeen, Tom hitchhiked around Europe, making money by playing his guitar in the streets.

In 1954, on his eighteenth birthday, Tom sailed to Alberta Canada and became a cowboy on the Alberta Ranch and then the A7 Ranch near Pincher Creek. Later he traveled to Hay River, North West Territories and worked as a fisherman on the Great Slave Lake, using nets through the ice. It was here, while fishing with a colleague that he was blown out into open waters on an ice flow. His friend died, but he survived being finally rescued by some trappers. He described his adventures in his book, *Beyond the Great Slave Lake.*

Back in England in 1956, Tom met and fell in love with Jeanine Arpourettes. They were married a year later in Paris and returned to Hay River, Canada, where they ran a fishing business together. Later they moved to Yellowknife, North West Territories, where Tom worked at the Giant gold mine and Jeanine worked in the local hospital.

In Yellowknife, Jeanine gave birth to their first son Tom, Junior in 1959 and Tom joined the Canadian Broadcasting Corporation as an announcer on CFYK.

Then in 1960 he became the CBC manager for a new radio station CBXH in Fort Smith, N.W.T., and stayed there until he returned to England as a CBC correspondent. Another son, Brodie, was born in London in 1961 and then Lionel was born in Scotland in 1962. Tom remained with the CBC until that day in 1964 when he met Ronan O'Rahilly and joined Radio Caroline.

After the outlawing of the pirate radio ships in 1967 by the Marine Offences Broadcasting Act, Tom worked as a disc-jockey for the BBC on the newly created BBC Radio 1, but soon decided to go back to Canada. He became a deejay on CHLO, St Thomas.

It was in London, Ontario that he formed the "Creative Arts Festival," with the participation of many local High School students, and also ran a drop-in youth center on Richmond street in London.

Then in 1970 he founded a creative program at Fanshawe College in London, Ontario, Canada, called "Creative Electronics," which after two years he converted into Music Industry Arts, a training program for recording engineers and record producers. This program is still active at the college.

When Radio Caroline began to broadcast legally in the 90s, he joined them for a time. Then in September 2004, he again went on the air with his son, Tom. He finally decided to retire from broadcasting and did his final Caroline show on April 8, 2007. Now Tom, Junior runs the show on Radio Caroline.

After nine years at Fanshawe College, he traveled to India, to pursue a long-standing interest and continue his search into Zen. This became his main focus. He was first a disciple of the Zen master Roshi Joshu Sasaki in California and then a disciple of Zen Master Osho in Poona, India. After Osho died in 1990, he became a disciple of Zen Master Mikaire.

After many years of meditation, on January 10, 1999, he had that experience which mystics call "Enlightenment." With Enlightenment, his name changed to Umi, Japanese for "the Sea." This caused people to form a Sangha, or community around him called Stillpoint, near Santa Cruz, California. He gives daily Satsangs and plays the clarinet and the lap steel guitar.